FutureChefs

FutureChefs

Recipes by Tomorrow's Cooks
Across the Nation and the World

RAMIN GANESHRAM

Photography by JEAN PAUL VELLOTTI

RODALE.

Rodale books may be purchased for business or promotional use or for special sales. For information,
please write to: Special Markets Department, Rodale Inc., 733 Third Avenue, New York, NY 10017.

Printed in the United States of America
Rodale Inc. makes every effort to use acid-free ♾, recycled paper ♻.

Book design by Christina Gaugler
Photographs by Jean Paul Vellotti

Library of Congress Cataloging-in-Publication Data is on file with the publisher.
ISBN-13: 978-1-62336-206-5

Distributed to the trade by Macmillan
2   4   6   8   10   9   7   5   3   1   paperback

We inspire and enable people to improve their lives and the world around them.
rodalebooks.com

*For Georgia and Donna
and
for Sophie Lollie, always*

Contents

Introduction

Four years ago I wrote what I thought was a fantastical piece of fiction about a 13-year-old chef who gets to participate in a competition cooking show on Food Network. Based on my own youthful fantasies of becoming a famous chef, I thought my premise in the middle-grade novel, *Stir It Up!*, was a neat bit of storytelling and nothing more.

But soon after the book was published, I found out how wrong I was. I started receiving emails, letters, tweets, and Facebook posts from kids who told me they were "just like the main character" and that they felt like I had told their life story in the pages of my book.

At first, I thought nothing of this early fan mail. The book, I thought with satisfaction, had found its niche. It wasn't until months—and then years—passed with letters still coming in that I started to really pay attention. Maybe these kid-chefs weren't a niche or an anomaly. Maybe they just were.

I decided to test this theory out and do a little digging. Were kid-chefs really that common? One of the first responses I got to my queries was from Alison Catanese. Her niece, Georgia, had turned her lifelong love of cooking to practical end when her mom died the year before and her dad suffered a stroke 2 months later. Georgia was 11.

I heard from the mom of young Tyler Trainer in Florida who was also 11 and couldn't get enough of being in the kitchen. His mom wasn't sure why, because neither she nor her husband liked to cook.

One young man I met, Rusty Schindler, spent the summer of his 16th year building a brick oven in his parents' backyard so he could bake bread with the wild yeast starter he had been keeping for a few months.

Young Eeshan Chakrabarti was the pickiest eater around—until he got on a step stool and started cooking for himself at age 6. Then there was Jack Witherspoon, who cooked to keep his mind off his leukemia treatments. Jack was 10 then. Since then, the 13-year-old has been on *The Tonight Show,* a contestant on Food Network's *Rachael vs. Guy,* and the author of his own cookbook. And Samantha Pecoraro, who is 16, can't even eat what she cooks, because of a rare medical condition.

The more kids I spoke with, the more stories emerged—too many to ignore as a passing fad. *FutureChefs* was born.

As I wrote this book, telling the stories of these young chefs, they became the teachers and I the student. I learned that while all of them are impressive, none are that unusual. Like their peers, they are being raised in a food-aware world where whole ingredients, respect for the earth and environment, and the desire to explore beyond their physical borders is the norm. These kids are vegetarians, farmers, travelers, activists, healthy eaters, and compassionate thinkers. And they are not alone.

While the stories you'll find in this book are dramatic and moving, exuberant and joyful, hopeful and determined, not every kid here is a cooking prodigy—in fact most aren't—but every story speaks to a deep and abiding passion for food.

And every story speaks to a generation poised to take back American Food from industry and restore it to its rightful place in home kitchens, in the fields of small farmers, and on the tables of everyone, regardless of income or education.

At first blush, it's easy to discount these young people as unusual in some way—oddities in "size small" chef's jackets or farmer's overalls—but nothing could be further from the truth. *FutureChefs* is just a taste of a vast network of people 18 and under who are poised to change the way we as Americans and as members of the international community think about, cook, and consume food.

Theirs is a way that honors the return to scratch cooking, the value of real food, and the importance of cultural connections. They are clear on how they want to see the food world evolve and they are taking action to make it so—to the ongoing benefit of us all.

More than anything, perhaps, these young chefs are the leaders of a new tomorrow. Consider them the forward flank of a changing American food scene that reflects the color and fabric of what we call our "national" food. Their love of real ingredients, their willingness to experiment with multiethnic flavor profiles, and their eye toward food justice and other issues of food reform are but a glimpse into a culinary future that they are changing with every step forward into tomorrow.

Ramin Ganeshram
Westport, Connecticut
August 2014

Acknowledgments

The greatest measure of my thanks goes to the young people who made this book possible with their amazing, inspiring, and sometimes astounding, stories of life in the kitchen.

Gratitude to Georgia Catanese and her dad, Joe, for the generosity of spirit they showed me by sharing Georgia's remarkable story when this book was merely a germ of an idea and allowing me to continue to share it with them through the years. Even more thanks go to Donna Catanese for raising such an extraordinary daughter. I never knew you, Donna, because you left this world too soon, but I thank you for all you've done.

My biggest cheerleader for this project has always been the inimitable Chef Kashia Cave, founder of My City Kitchen. Thank you for your faith and for helping to test the recipes in this book with your amazing group of teen chefs: John Alvarez, Jonathan Ancrum, Ebony Brown, Alana Brown, Tiera Burch, Randy McKinney, and Alex Woodworth.

Testing thanks also goes to Chef Cecily Gans and the class of 2014 culinary team at Staples High School in my hometown of Westport, Connecticut: Zachary Reiser, Sarah Rountree, Allyssa McGahern, Rayna Weiser, Nathan Francis, and Cecilia Kiker. And to Chef Bob McIntosh and his students at the Concord Regional Technical Center in New Hampshire: Michael Filides, Henry Hochberg, Daiquiri Przybyla, Randi Houle, Jeremy Kelly, Damian Woodard, and Samantha Bruce.

To my dear friends Victoria Kann and Renee Brown: Thanks for always offering your encouragement, your time, your help, and your strong shoulders to lean on. Thank you to my husband Jean Paul Vellotti for taking beautiful pictures and for cheerfully being pressed into tasting service for this and my other books.

And last, but never ever least, thank you to my daughter, Sophia, through whose eyes I have been blessed to experience both the magic and wonder of childhood and the possibilities for a brighter future, every single day.

CHAPTER 1

Great Beginnings

(Soups/Salads)

The most common meal starters, soups and salads, hold a particular place in our American hearts. Warming, comforting soup calls to mind a sense of home and hearth. Perhaps this is why kids are often the most beloved spokespeople in canned soup commercials from time immemorial. The recipes in this chapter tell another story: Young people are no longer the passive recipients of a simple bowl of soup. Instead, here they act as creators, building each spoonful on a foundation of fresh and wholesome ingredients. So, too, the salads in this chapter demonstrate that not only do today's youngsters appreciate fresh, raw vegetables and greens, but they know how to use them to best advantage. What you'll find is a diversity of preparations in terms of ingredients and complexity. Represented in this chapter are both soups and salads that eat like meals as well as those that are tantalizing openers to a larger menu.

KEY: GF Gluten Free   VG Vegan   V Vegetarian

Mazy Wirt Hanson
Des Moines, Iowa

Mazian Hanson's goal is to write 1,000 posts on his food blog *Mazy's Food Adventures,* where he explores adventurous eating. The 9-year-old food blogger, whose nickname is Mazy, got inspired to visit restaurants and write about new and different dishes specifically to influence other kids to be more open to new foods. The self-styled "adventurous eater" says he's tried and likes American, Indian, Japanese, Chinese, Mexican, Vietnamese, Salvadoran, and Greek food to name some, but sushi is his favorite.

"I will try anything. I have friends who are picky eaters. I try to get them to eat other foods," he says. Part of his trying anything spirit is an annual visit to the World Food & Music Festival in Mazy's hometown of Des Moines where multiple countries are represented with their national dishes. At this year's festival Mazy tried pork belly from America, goat burgers from the Philippines, kimchi tacos from Korea, blood soup from El Salvador, and gelato ice cream from Italy.

When Mazy cooks at home, he opts for simple, fresh recipes. One favorite is **Egg Drop Soup,** which he tried while searching for a soup he might like. "I added shredded carrots to the recipe because I really like the way carrots taste and the bright orange makes the soup more colorful. I like to put it in a thermos and take it to school for lunch, which always gets my friends interested because it's something new." The recipe was also appealing to Mazy because of its semi-exotic nature—particularly the technique of creating scrambled egg "ribbons" in the soup, which come out beautifully with a little patience and a steady hand.

EGG DROP SOUP

SERVES 4 TO 6

1 teaspoon toasted sesame oil
½ cup shredded carrots
2 scallions, finely chopped
1 clove garlic, minced
4 cups chicken stock or reduced-sodium chicken broth
1 tablespoon soy sauce
2 eggs, well beaten
Celery leaves, for garnish (optional)
Red pepper flakes, for garnish (optional)

1. In a deep saucepan, heat the sesame oil over medium-low heat. Add the carrots, scallions, and garlic and stir well. Cook for 1 minute. Do not allow the ingredients to brown.

2. Pour in the chicken stock and soy sauce. Mix well and simmer for 10 minutes.

3. Stirring constantly, pour in the beaten eggs, so that they form long "ribbons" as they cook. Once all the eggs are added, stop stirring and simmer for 1 minute more.

4. Serve hot, garnished with celery leaves and red pepper flakes to taste, if desired.

Ezra Steinberg
Mountain View, California

It's only natural that you'd start cooking at age 4 if your dad got his start as a restaurant baker. While still a preschooler, Ezra Steinberg's repertoire mostly included eggs and experimentation. "I just threw a lot of stuff together and it sort of came out *blech*," he says of one of his early soups, a preparation around which he's now developed finesse. Now, at the mature age of 6, Ezra does most of the shopping, creation, and preparation of his original soups himself—with help from Mom and Dad only when necessary. His **Rescue Soup** was created, he says, "to rescue people from bad flavors," and is highly focused on the bounty from his family's and school's seasonal gardens—the places where Ezra first learns about most of his new ingredients. When it came to this soup, Ezra's dad, Daniel, was wary of his son's particular combination of vegetables, but was pleasantly surprised when it was done.

You can experiment with your own favorite vegetables, but keep in mind that firm-fleshed vegetables will work best. You may also want to increase the garlic, salt, or pepper to your own taste. Serve with Rosemary Bread without the dipping sauce (page 192).

RESCUE SOUP

SERVES 4 TO 6

2 medium red bell peppers

1 medium Japanese eggplant

1 tablespoon olive oil

1 medium leek, roughly chopped

6 white mushrooms, roughly chopped

6 shiitake mushrooms, stems discarded, caps roughly chopped

2 cloves garlic, chopped

¼ teaspoon minced fresh rosemary

4 cups vegetable stock or water

½ teaspoon coarse salt

Freshly ground black pepper

1 porcini bouillon cube (optional)

1. Preheat the broiler.

2. Place the bell peppers and eggplant on a lightly greased baking pan. Broil the peppers and eggplant until the skins are browned and blistered, 10 to 15 minutes. Turn the vegetables during cooking so that all sides are well browned. Set the peppers and eggplant aside to cool.

3. When cool enough to handle, slice the eggplant in half and scoop the flesh into a food processor (or blender). Discard the skin and stem. Seed, stem, and peel the red peppers. The skin should peel away easily. Rinse the peppers to remove any clinging skin, if need be. Add to the food processor (or blender). Set aside.

4. Heat a large skillet over medium heat and add the olive oil. Add the leek, mushrooms, and garlic and cook until the garlic and mushrooms are lightly browned, 5 to 7 minutes. Add the rosemary and stir well. Cook for 1 minute more.

5. Add the cooked leek mixture and ¼ cup of the vegetable stock or water to the food processor (or blender). Puree until all the ingredients form a smooth, loose paste without lumps. Add more stock, as needed, to achieve this consistency.

6. Pour the pureed vegetable mixture into a 4-quart saucepan or medium soup pot and add the remaining stock or water. Add the salt, black pepper to taste, and the porcini bouillon cube (if using). Stir well and return to the stove.

7. Simmer the soup over medium-low heat for 15 minutes to allow the flavors to combine. Serve hot with Rosemary Bread (page 192).

Cheyenne Preston
Milwaukee, Wisconsin

Cheynne Preston is a senior at Milwaukee's Escuela Verde, a charter school for students interested in sustainability, student-led learning, and restorative justice. Cheyenne volunteers in the Lunch Bunch—a committee of students and teachers who facilitate lunch deliveries from local businesses. The school does not have its own kitchen and sources food from outside restaurants. The task is challenging because Escuela Verde is a vegetarian school in a neighborhood struggling with urban blight, and where many of the students are considered "at-risk."

Cooking is the 17-year-old's main area of focus and she plans to make a series of videos teaching other young people about healthy food choices for her senior thesis. "There are many people who are eating fast food because they don't know that eating healthy food can be just as cost-efficient and easy to make," she says. "I want to make a series of YouTube videos showing how to make recipes that are available as snacks and food everyone can make."

Cheyenne's natural curiosity extends far beyond her actual borders. The teen has a love of Asian foods and of cosplay, where people dress up as anime or other characters from a show or a book. She mentions being especially influenced by an episode of her favorite Korean television series *Boys Over Flowers*. "There was a scene where the characters Jun-pyo and Jan-di ate a platter of fatty tuna," says Cheyenne. "The dish was so complicated and beautiful that it was an eye popper."

Cheyenne spends a lot of time exploring and learning about new foods. This **Vegetarian Ramen** is inspired by her walks through Asian markets. The teen hopes, one day, to open her own cosplay cafe where she can marry both the culinary and cultural aspects of Japanese, Korean, and other Asian communities.

VEGETARIAN RAMEN

SERVES 4

- 2 teaspoons dried wakame
- 3 eggs
- 2¼ cups white whole wheat flour, plus more for dusting
- 1 teaspoon salt
- 3 cups Kombu Dashi (recipe opposite)
- 3 tablespoons yellow miso paste
- 6 ounces firm tofu, cut into small cubes
- 1 scallion, thinly sliced
- Toasted sesame oil, for serving (optional)
- Chili oil, for serving (optional)

1. In a small bowl, combine the wakame and ⅓ cup water. Set aside.

2. In a bowl, mix together the eggs, flour, and 3 tablespoons water. Using your hands, knead the dough until stiff. It should not be sticky. If the dough is sticky, gradually dust it with flour and continue to knead until it is firm. If the dough is too dry, add water by sprinkling it on top of the dough and kneading until it is stiff but not sticky. Wrap the dough in a damp paper towel and allow to rest for 30 minutes to 1 hour.

3. When the dough has rested, dust a clean work surface with flour and dust the dough with flour as well. Roll out the dough to a rough rectangle about 13 × 15 inches and about ⅛ inch thick. Continue dusting the dough lightly, as needed, to prevent the rolling pin from sticking to it.

4. Starting at a short end, fold the dough over twice. Sprinkle with more flour. Using a sharp knife, cut the dough roll crosswise into ⅛-inch-wide noodles. Unfold each noodle gently.

5. In a large saucepan, bring 4 cups water and the salt to a boil. Add the noodles and use chopsticks to gently stir the noodles around until they float, about 4 minutes.

6. In a separate large saucepan, stir together the Kombu Dashi and miso and place over medium heat. Stir until the miso dissolves. Add the tofu, reduce the soup to a slight simmer, and cook until just heated, do not boil.

7. Strain the wakame and divide it and the scallion evenly among 4 soup bowls. Divide the cooked noodles among the bowls and then pour the soup over them. Gently stir, using chopsticks. Serve hot, drizzled with toasted sesame oil and chili oil, if desired.

Kombu Dashi

MAKES 4 CUPS

Dashi is the broth that is an underpinning for many Japanese soups—noodle and otherwise. Mastering dashi is foundational to well-rounded flavor. While traditional dashi is most often made with dried bonito tuna flakes, this vegetarian version uses kombu seaweed. If you like more intense flavor, you can increase the amount of kombu to 2 sheets for the same amount of water.

1 sheet dried kombu
4 cups water

1. Clean the kombu by wiping with a slightly damp paper towel. Slice the kombu into thin strips.

2. Place the kombu in a medium bowl with the water. Cover and set aside for at least 10 hours and up to 24.

3. Set a sieve over a bowl and drain the kombu soaking liquid into the bowl. Discard the kombu pieces. This mixture can keep, refrigerated, for up to 1 week.

Sophie Trachtenberg
Oklahoma City, Oklahoma

At 15, Sophie Trachtenberg is already the keeper of her family's European Jewish heritage. A self-styled "storyteller through food," Sophie took over baking her great-aunt Leona's mandelbrot, a Jewish cookie not unlike biscotti. "Aunt Leona is a remarkable family member of mine who fled to the United States before the Holocaust, but her sisters and mother were killed in the Warsaw Ghetto. Making this recipe revives part of our family history," says Sophie. When she's not playing basketball for her Oklahoma City high school team or volunteering for Cleats for Kids, a local charity that collects and distributes sporting equipment to youngsters in need, Sophie is working on her food blog *Simply Sophie Bea* and taking advanced cooking classes. Part of her ongoing passion for her family history was realized when she mastered her great-grandmother Evelyn's **Matzoh Ball Soup,** a staple at the family's New Year table.

Although matzoh ball soup is a traditional Jewish staple, it's a preparation that requires some finesse, and Sophie practiced her version many times before it became the showcase of the holiday spread. A long, slow simmer is key to the most flavorful chicken broth and a light hand is required when mixing the matzoh balls. Resist the urge to overbeat the batter or your resulting matzoh balls will be "sinkers" rather than "floaters."

MATZOH BALL SOUP
SERVES 4 TO 6

Broth

- ½ chicken (about 2 pounds)
- ½ medium white onion, chopped
- 1 carrot, chopped
- 1 stalk celery, chopped
- 1 parsnip, chopped
- ½ bunch parsley
- 1 sprig fresh dill

Matzoh balls

- 1 cup matzoh meal
- 2 eggs, well beaten
- 3 tablespoons vegetable oil
- 3 tablespoons chopped fresh parsley

- 1 tablespoon chopped fresh dill
  Salt and freshly ground black pepper

Soup

- ½ medium white onion, cut into ½-inch pieces
- 3 carrots, cut into ½-inch pieces
- 2 stalks celery, cut into ½-inch pieces
- 1 parsnip, cut into ½-inch pieces
- ½ bunch parsley, chopped
- 1 tablespoon chopped fresh dill
  Salt and freshly ground black pepper

  Cooked egg noodles, for serving (optional)

1. For the broth: In a deep stockpot, bring 3 quarts (12 cups) water to a boil. Add the chicken and simmer over medium heat, skimming the fat from the top as needed. Once there is no fat left to skim, about 45 minutes to 1 hour, add the onion, carrot, celery, parsnip, parsley, and dill. Simmer on medium-low for 1 hour, uncovered.

2. Meanwhile, for the matzoh balls: In a medium bowl, mix the matzo meal with ¼ cup water, the eggs, vegetable oil, parsley, dill, and a pinch each of salt and pepper. Stir until just combined, do not overmix. Put the matzoh ball mixture into the refrigerator and chill for 20 minutes.

3. In a large pot, combine 3 quarts (12 cups) water and 1 tablespoon salt and bring to a boil over high heat.

4. After the matzoh ball mixture has chilled, remove it from the refrigerator. To avoid sticking, spray some cooking spray or add a bit of oil to your hands before forming the matzoh balls. Scoop about ¼ cup of mixture and roll it into a ball between your palms. Repeat until all the mixture is used up, you should have 8 or 9 small matzoh balls.

5. Drop the matzoh balls into the boiling water and boil for 10 minutes. Reduce the heat to low and simmer for another 20 minutes. Once the matzo balls are fluffy and rise to the top of the pot, remove them from the water with a slotted spoon and set aside.

6. By now the chicken broth will be ready to be strained. Remove the chicken and set aside to cool for 15 minutes. Strain the broth into a large saucepan. Discard the vegetables and herbs. Once the chicken is cool enough to handle, remove the skin and the bones and shred the meat into bite-size pieces.

7. For the soup: Add the chicken, onion, carrots, celery, parsnip, parsley, and dill to the broth in the saucepan. Stir in salt and pepper to taste and simmer until the vegetables are tender, about 30 minutes.

8. Add the finished matzoh balls to the soup and simmer until they are warmed through, about 5 minutes. Serve with egg noodles, if desired. Add salt and pepper to taste.

Karthik Rohatgi
Reno, Nevada

This 15-year-old crusader focuses his talents on helping the poorest residents of his city access fresh produce. Karthik, who attends an academy for extremely gifted children in Reno, first focused on feeding those less fortunate as a grade schooler when, during Halloween, he passed on the candy and asked, instead, for money and canned goods to donate to the Food Bank of Northern Nevada. On one of his weekly food drops to the organization, he realized that fresh produce was never among the foods distributed to those in need of the service. In January 2011, Karthik enlisted the help of advisers from his school to create Farm Fresh for Kids whose goal is to fight childhood obesity and obesity-related illnesses by providing access to fresh food via farmers' market vouchers and nutrition education through low-income clinics in his area. In 2013 he presented a TEDTalk in Reno about the initiative. A vegetarian for sustainability and health reasons, Karthik, who calls himself a "passionate environmentalist," is dedicated to growing foods in his home garden and experimenting with produce to come up with new recipes, such as this butternut squash soup.

Smooth and creamy, Karthik's **Butternut Squash Kale Soup** can be made vegan by substituting coconut oil for the butter. Serve the soup with Gluten-Free Sun-Dried Tomato Muffins (page 187).

BUTTERNUT SQUASH KALE SOUP

SERVES 4 TO 6

1 medium butternut squash
1 tablespoon butter, at room temperature
3 tablespoons olive oil
1 large onion, finely chopped
5 or 6 cloves garlic, minced
3 sprigs of fresh thyme
1 tablespoon chopped fresh parsley
2 tablespoons all-purpose flour
5 to 6 cups vegetable stock
12 cups baby kale, chopped
1 teaspoon salt
½ teaspoon freshly ground pepper
2 teaspoons dark brown sugar

1. Preheat the oven to 400°F. Line a baking sheet with foil.

2. Halve the butternut squash lengthwise and scoop out the seeds and any loose fiber. Lightly coat the cut faces with the softened butter. Place cut side down on the baking sheet and bake until a knife goes through the skin easily, 1 hour to 1 hour 30 minutes. Let the squash cool completely, then scoop out the flesh and set aside. Discard the skin.

3. In large, deep saucepan, heat the olive oil over medium heat. Add the onion and cook

until translucent, 3 to 4 minutes. Add the garlic, thyme, and parsley and cook for 1 minute more.

4. Add the flour and cook, stirring, for 1 minute. Slowly add 2 cups of the stock, stirring constantly. Add the baked butternut squash and stir well. Stir in the remaining stock and simmer for 10 minutes. Remove from the heat.

5. Use a hand blender to puree the soup in the pan until it's smooth. (Alternatively, in batches, puree the soup in a blender and then return to the pan.)

6. Return the soup to medium heat and bring to a boil. Add the kale, salt, pepper, and sugar. Simmer until the kale is tender, 5 to 10 minutes. Serve hot.

Safiyah Riddle
New York, New York

Along with her best friend and fellow vegetarian, Sadie Hope-Gund (page 260), Safiyah Riddle is a star of the documentary *What's On Your Plate?*, which chronicles a year spent exploring where food comes from and why people eat what they do. The movie, by Emmy Award–winning filmmaker Catherine Gund, follows 12- and 13-year-old girls as they learn about issues ranging from nutrition, to organic versus conventional farming, to the politics behind school food and what "local" really means.

Now 17, Safiyah credits her parents' exclusion of meat and processed food from their home and her grandmother Jane Russell's cooking as her strongest early influences in the kitchen.

"Being a vegetarian for my entire life has certainly forced me to be creative when it comes to protein substitutes," she says. "Additionally, growing up in New York City has allowed me to mix and match different flavors from different regions, without subscribing to one particular ethnic style."

Even though she will be attending college soon, she says that the impact of her middle school participation in *What's On Your Plate* will always be an influence in her life.

"As early as kindergarten I became aware that I did not eat the same things everyone else did," she says. "Then, I was given the unique opportunity to explore the food that is often just put in front of us kids without any explanation."

Exploring healthy eating options and various eating styles has given Safiyah the confidence to adapt old favorites to her own taste. Her **Cayenne Cheddar Potato Soup** is a riff on her grandmother's signature potato soup that she has on any visit to her grandmother's Chester Springs, Pennsylvania, home. Safiyah's adaptation features cayenne and black pepper, which adds another level of depth and flavor to this thick and hearty soup. If cheddar cheese is not to your taste, you may substitute any yellow cheese such as Colby or Monterey jack. Serve with Rosemary Bread without the dipping sauce (page 192) if desired.

(continued)

CAYENNE CHEDDAR POTATO SOUP

- 3 tablespoons butter
- 2 medium onions, chopped
- ¼ cup all-purpose flour
- 6 cups vegetable broth
- 4 cups peeled, diced potatoes
- 2 cups shredded cheddar cheese
- 2 teaspoons cayenne pepper (or more to taste)
- ½ teaspoon salt (or more to taste)
  Freshly ground black pepper

1. In a large saucepan, melt the butter over medium-low heat. Add the onions and cook until softened and just beginning to brown, 5 to 7 minutes.

2. Add the flour and stir for 1 minute, then gradually add the broth while continuing to stir. Bring to a boil for 30 seconds, then reduce the heat to a simmer. Add the potatoes, cover, and simmer until the potatoes can easily be mashed, about 20 minutes. Remove the pan from the heat.

3. Using a potato masher or the back of a large spoon, mash the potatoes in the broth. (Alternatively you may strain the potatoes from the pot using a slotted spoon and puree then in a blender or food processor. Return the pureed potatoes to the broth, and mix well.)

4. Stir in the cheddar until it melts. Add the cayenne, salt, and black pepper to taste and stir very well. Serve hot.

Romilly Newman
New York, New York

Cooking is not what people in Romilly Newman's family generally do, even though the 15-year-old New Yorker describes her kin as universally passionate eaters of good food. It was then 9-year-old Romilly's obsession with watching the Food Network that encouraged her to try her own hand at creating beautiful food.

"I sat in front of the TV for hours on end and marveled at how much fun the chefs were having and how beautiful the food looked, and that was when I realized that I wanted to pursue cooking," says Romilly, who chronicles her experiences on her blog *Little Girl in the Kitchen*. That pursuit has led her to be a guest on the *Today* show, NPR, and one of the youngest competitor to date on Food Network's *Chopped*.

Even though she's already achieved more than many cooks twice her age, Romilly knows that her cooking style is a work in progress. "I'm still very young, so my food is constantly evolving. As I get older I find my food and flavor profiles going in different and exciting directions. I really love how expressive and creative cooking is and as a young chef I think it's really important not to take my cooking too seriously," she says. "While I care a tremendous amount about what I make, I still think it's okay to sometimes go in the kitchen and do extremely unconventional things and just play around with flavors, textures, and elements." Romilly's **Shaved Snow Pea & Mint Salad** is an example of what she calls one of her "seasonal signature" dishes—created from what inspires her most from locally harvested bounty. Although, this dish is simple, its fresh flavors carry it to a level of sophistication that makes it a perfect starter for any summer or winter menu. Because the salad is easy to prepare, Romilly suggests making it just before serving so that the sliced mint does not darken and wilt.

(continued)

SHAVED SNOW PEA & MINT SALAD

1 pound snow peas

Grated zest and juice of 1 large lemon

¼ cup extra virgin olive oil

2 tablespoons finely sliced fresh mint, plus more for garnish

Sea salt and coarsely ground black pepper

¼ pound Parmesan or Asiago cheese

1. Trim peas by gently pulling the thin string from the stem end of each pea pod down the length of the pea. Discard. If needed, trim the stem end of the snow peas as well and then slice each pea pod thinly into slivers. Place the sliced pea pods in a medium bowl and set aside.

2. In a separate small bowl, combine the lemon zest and juice. Slowly whisk in the olive oil. Stir in the mint and salt and pepper to taste.

3. Pour the dressing over the peas and toss well, making sure that all of the peas are well coated in the dressing.

4. Using a cheese slicer or sharp paring knife, cut thin slices of the Parmesan and sprinkle over the top of the salad. Garnish with additional sliced mint, if desired.

Nam Pla (Thai Fish Sauce)

Fermented fish sauce is a foundational ingredient in Thai cuisine as well as other Southeast Asian nations. Thai fish sauce (called *nam pla*) has a strong, salty flavor with meaty undertones. When used in the right proportions it can add well-rounded flavor to even raw preparations such as Amber Kelley's Refreshing Thai Cucumber Salad. When experimenting with *nam pla*, less is always more. Add this flavoring to dishes sparingly, increasing the amount incrementally until you achieve the intensity that is right for you. *Nam pla* pairs well with spicy and sour flavors.

Amber Kelley
Woodinville, Washington

With two parents who are wellness coaches, Amber Kelley has never eaten anything but clean, healthy food, so it took the 10-year-old a little while to understand that other kids didn't necessarily eat the way she did. Her response to her newfound knowledge was to start an online cooking show featuring recipes she thinks other young people might be encouraged to try. "I want to show other kids that it's cool to be healthy. There are always healthier options that are just as yummy, or even MORE yummy!" says Amber. "And on top of it, cooking is super fun and if you cook your own foods, it's even easier to be healthy. That's a double win!"

The young cook was one of the winners of First Lady Michelle Obama's 2013 Healthy Lunchtime Challenge created in concert with Epicurious.com. Amber represented her state with a no-noodle lasagna made with zucchini "pasta" and attended the White House Kids' "State Dinner" with the First Lady and President Obama. Amber created this salad as a way to introduce other people her age to the pungent yet fresh flavors of traditional Thai foods. Her **Refreshing Thai Cucumber Salad** is a good example of a dish that can please everyone with its balanced mix of sweet, spicy, and hot notes.

REFRESHING THAI CUCUMBER SALAD

SERVES 4

Dressing

- 2 tablespoons nam pla (Thai fish sauce)
- Juice of ½ lime
- 1 tablespoon soy sauce
- 1 clove garlic, minced
- ¼ teaspoon cayenne pepper (or to taste)
- 1½ teaspoons brown sugar (or to taste)

Salad

- 1 English cucumber, chopped into small cubes
- ¼ cup finely diced red bell pepper
- 2 scallions, thinly sliced
- 1 shallot, minced
- ½ cup chopped fresh cilantro
- ¼ cup roughly chopped dry-roasted Valencia peanuts, for garnish

1. For the dressing: In a small bowl, whisk together the nam pla, lime juice, soy sauce, garlic, cayenne, and brown sugar. Whisk well until the sugar is entirely dissolved.

2. For the salad: In a large salad bowl, toss together the cucumber, bell pepper, scallions, shallot, and cilantro. Pour the dressing over the salad a little at a time, mixing well between additions.

3. Garnish with the chopped peanuts.

Sophia Hampton
Westport, Connecticut

As vice president of her high school's culinary club, Sophia Hampton spends the first Friday of every month with her clubmates cooking for the Gillespie Center, a homeless shelter in Westport, Connecticut.

The 16-year-old is also the features editor for her school's newspaper, where she finds she has made a transition from writing mostly about fashion to writing mostly about cooking. "Food has always played a major role in my life, but only recently have I thought that maybe instead of fashion I would like to combine food and journalism," Sophia says. "I get so much more fulfillment out of cooking and creating a meal than I get out of putting together an outfit."

The high school junior says this change of outlook came most recently while working as the intern for this book. "It's easy to lose faith in the younger generation's eating habits because of the products we consume. Every time someone buys Doritos or Coke, a part of me cringes," she says. "However, clicking through various recipes, ideas, and food blogs has shown me that there is a whole generation of young foodies that is budding and flourishing. It's so exciting that it gives me so much hope for the future of food."

Sophia first started experimenting with kale as a substitute for romaine lettuce in her **Kale Caesar Salad** because she suspected the hardy green's stronger flavor would better stand up to the anchovy paste and garlic that she likes to use liberally. Kale, she says, doesn't wilt as easily as romaine and provides a better springboard for the creamy, intense, Caesar dressing.

(continued)

KALE CAESAR SALAD

Dressing

1 to 2 garlic cloves (or more to taste)

4 anchovy fillets, plus 1 tablespoon of their oil

2 tablespoons lemon juice

1 teaspoon Worcestershire sauce

3 tablespoons mayonnaise

½ cup extra-virgin olive oil

Salt and freshly ground black pepper

Salad

Cooking spray

1 or 2 strips turkey bacon (optional)

1 bunch Tuscan kale (aka lacinato kale), roughly chopped

1 hard-boiled egg, sliced

¼ cup grated Parmesan cheese

1. For the dressing: In a mortar and pestle, pound the garlic, anchovies, and anchovy oil into a paste. Scrape this mixture into a small bowl and whisk in the lemon juice, Worcestershire sauce, and mayonnaise until emulsified. Whisk in the olive oil. Season with salt and pepper to taste.

2. For the salad: If using turkey bacon, coat a skillet lightly with cooking spray and cook the bacon over medium heat until crisp, about 5 minutes. Drain the turkey bacon on a plate lined with paper towels. When cool, crumble the turkey bacon into small pieces.

3. Place the chopped kale in a large bowl and pour the dressing over it. Add the egg and Parmesan. If using, sprinkle with the crumbled bacon.

Madeline Dalton
Newcastle, Washington

Unrefined but not without panache is the way to describe 15-year-old Madeline Dalton's cooking style. The author of the blog *Teens Can Cook, Too!* has focused her cooking on ingredients that are minimally processed ever since taking a healthy cooking challenge at a local natural foods market.

"I took a 28-day challenge and omitted dairy, eggs, meat, refined grains, refined sugars, and refined oils from my diet. Even though this seems extreme, it opened my mind to just how many things you can make with only the healthiest of ingredients," says Madeline. "While I don't think that it is necessarily a practical way to live your everyday life, it has definitely helped me police myself when I create recipes. Now, more than ever, I try to use little to no oil, dairy, or sugar in my recipes; but I'm a growing teenager and I realize that eating ice cream now and then won't kill me."

Madeline counts recipe creation as the part of cooking she enjoys most, beginning when she re-created the recipes in several teen cookbooks she received as a youngster. Her **Black Bean & Corn Salad** calls for raw corn, so make sure you use the freshest, ripest—and preferably organic—corn you can find. Avocados add creaminess to the recipe in the absence of oil in the dressing, and depending on your love—or not—of cilantro, you may want to up or reduce the amount of this pungent herb.

Serve with greens as a luncheon salad or as a side dish for grilled meats or fish.

(continued)

BLACK BEAN & CORN SALAD

SERVES 4 TO 6

1 cup dried black beans or 1 can (15 ounces) black beans

1 ear of corn, shucked

2 medium tomatoes, diced

2 avocados, diced

¼ cup finely chopped fresh cilantro

Juice of 1 lime

½ teaspoon cayenne pepper

Salt and freshly ground black pepper

1. If using dried beans, soak the beans overnight in 3 cups water. Drain the beans and combine in a saucepan with 3 cups fresh water. Bring to a boil, then reduce to a simmer and cook until the beans are tender, about 40 minutes. Drain and transfer to a large bowl. (If using canned beans, drain beans into a sieve, rinse well, and transfer to the bowl.)

2. Carefully cut off the stem so the bottom end of the ear of corn will sit flat. Holding the corn upright, slice the corn kernels off the cob from top to bottom, working your way around the cob until all the kernels are removed.

3. Add the corn to the bowl along with the tomatoes, avocados, cilantro, lime juice, cayenne, and salt and black pepper to taste. Gently mix so you do not mash the avocado. Adjust the seasonings if needed.

Using Dried Beans

Dried beans are an economical—and some say tastier—substitute for canned. With the exception of softer beans such as lentils or split peas, the rule of thumb for all dried beans is the same: Soak the beans in three times their volume of cold water overnight. For example, 1 cup of beans would be soaked in 3 cups of water. Drain the soaked beans and discard the water. Bring fresh water (3 times the volume of water to beans) to a boil. Add the drained beans and simmer until the beans are just tender, 30 to 40 minutes. Use them immediately in cooked or raw preparations such as salads, or freeze them in zip-top bags to use later. Never salt beans while they are cooking or the skins will become tough.

Elliot Martin
Chicago, Illinois

The Edible Garden at the Farm-in-the-Zoo at Chicago's Lincoln Park Zoo is a favorite hangout for 8-year-old Elliot Martin. Not just a pleasant spot to spend a few hours, the farm and garden became the inspiration for Elliot to give up eating meat when he was 4 years old. "Once I realized that the chicken that my mom made was the same as the chicken at the Farm-in-the-Zoo, I didn't want to eat chicken anymore and became a vegetarian," he says.

His beliefs have lead the young man to grow his own vegetables and become a mentor to children even younger than himself. Elliot's particular brand of food-centered microactivism also means taking a larger world-view and sharing it with his peers. As an animal advocate, he keeps other grade schoolers in the know about the impacts of food production on international ecologies. Palm oil is on his list of no-nos because its harvest damages the habitat of orangutans. In kid-speak, that means a large number of packaged favorites—like Oreos—are off the list.

"I'm not sure how much of an influence I have on my classmates," he says, "but at least at school the other kids are always interested in what I'm eating. Some of the teachers are too."

Elliot favors simple foods that allow the natural flavor to shine through. Yet, he acknowledges, when using relatively few ingredients those ingredients have to be the best you can find. He first created his version of **Caprese Salad** as a way to use the abundant tomatoes he grows. Although he says that the recipe is best with those you grow yourself, those grown at a local farm will serve just as well. For the best result, look for ripe tomatoes that are firm and unbruised. While eye-popping red tomatoes make for a dramatic presentation, he encourages experimenting with the many varieties and colors of tomatoes out there to experience the subtle difference in taste that different cultivars provide.

CAPRESE SALAD
SERVES 4

2 large tomatoes, cut into 6 to 8 wedges each

½ pound fresh mozzarella, cut into bite-size chunks

6 to 10 large fresh basil leaves, torn or cut into a chiffonade (see "Making a Chiffonade" on page 116)

Extra virgin olive oil, as needed

Sea salt and freshly cracked black pepper

1. Arrange the tomatoes on a plate and add the fresh mozzarella.

2. Sprinkle the basil leaves on top and drizzle with extra virgin olive oil according to your taste.

3. Season with sea salt and freshly cracked pepper to taste.

Cole Malouin
Redondo Beach, California

"I'm a science geek—and proud of it," says Cole Malouin, who, at 14, is most interested in engineering and robotics. When he's not trying to encourage other kids toward STEM (Science, Technology, Engineering, and Mathematics) pursuits, he explores the science of cooking. In 2013 Cole was a contestant on the Food Network show *Rachael vs. Guy* featuring kid chefs competing on teams with Food Network celebrities Rachael Ray and Guy Fieri.

On set Cole was considered the "teen Alton Brown" because of his love of experimenting in the kitchen. "I'm interested in exploring molecular gastronomy next," he says—a new field of culinary science he'll have to fit in between volunteering for school and charity events, including cooking demonstrations geared toward other teens.

"When kids learn to cook, they learn about math, science, and health. Plus, I also try to talk about the history of the food," he says. "Cooking is a good teacher in the sense that if you mess up and it tastes horrible, you won't do that again."

Cole particularly likes to build composed salads to prove that a salad can be made with as much technique and skill as a main course. His **Quinoa Salad with Fire-Roasted Pepper Sauce** is deliberately designed to be a full meal in itself, thanks to the protein density in the grain.

QUINOA SALAD WITH FIRE-ROASTED PEPPER SAUCE

SERVES 4 TO 6 AS MAIN OR
8 TO 10 AS A STARTER

Vinaigrette

- ¼ cup champagne vinegar
- 2 tablespoons balsamic vinegar
- ¾ cup extra virgin olive oil
- 1 tablespoon finely chopped fresh parsley
- 1 tablespoon finely chopped fresh basil
- 1 clove garlic, finely chopped
- ¼ teaspoon salt
- ¼ teaspoon freshly ground black pepper

Salad

- 3 cups vegetable stock
- 3 cloves garlic, finely chopped
- 4 tablespoons finely chopped fresh parsley
- 1 cup quinoa, rinsed well in a fine-mesh sieve
- 2 or 3 orange bell peppers, diced
- ¼ jicama, peeled and diced (to equal about ½ cup)

1 English cucumber, diced (optional)

¼ medium red onion, diced

 Grated zest of 1 lemon

 Salt and freshly ground black pepper

 Butter lettuce leaves, for the platter

½ cup Fire-Roasted Pepper Sauce (recipe follows)

1. For the vinaigrette: In a food processor, combine the champagne and balsamic vinegars, olive oil, parsley, basil, garlic, salt, and pepper and pulse until the ingredients are well incorporated and emulsified. Set aside.

2. For the salad: In a large saucepan, combine the vegetable stock, garlic, and 2 tablespoons of the parsley and bring to a boil. Add the quinoa, stir well, and reduce the heat to a simmer. Simmer the quinoa uncovered until all the liquid is absorbed and the quinoa grains begin to burst open, about 30 minutes.

3. Let the quinoa cool completely, then mix in the bell peppers, jicama, cucumber (if using), onion, lemon zest, and remaining 2 tablespoons parsley. Dress the quinoa salad with the vinaigrette, add salt and black pepper to taste, and stir well. Refrigerate.

4. Layer a platter with the butter lettuce leaves and spoon the quinoa mixture over them. Drizzle the fire-roasted pepper sauce over the quinoa and serve.

Fire-Roasted Pepper Sauce   MAKES 1½ CUPS

This fire-roasted pepper sauce is both sweet and tangy without being overpowering. While Cole Malouin developed the sauce for the quinoa salad (opposite), it is equally good as an all-purpose salad dressing or as a light sauce for sautéed or grilled chicken or fish.

2 large red bell peppers

 Extra virgin olive oil, for brushing

1 medium yellow bell pepper, halved

1 tomato, quartered and seeded

 Juice of ½ lemon

2 tablespoons olive oil

1 tablespoon champagne vinegar

1 teaspoon sea salt

1 teaspoon freshly ground black pepper

1. Preheat the oven to 450°F.

2. Lightly brush the red bell peppers with extra virgin olive oil. Place on a baking sheet or in a baking dish and roast until the skin is blackened and blistered, turning once or twice while cooking to ensure that all sides are charred, about 30 minutes. When the peppers are cool enough to handle, gently pull out stem and seeds and peel away the skin. Rinse away any clinging seeds, if needed.

3. In a blender, combine the roasted red peppers, the yellow bell pepper, tomato, lemon juice, olive oil, and champagne vinegar and puree until smooth, about 1 minute. Season with the salt and black pepper.

CHAPTER 2

Snack Attack

(Apps/Snacks)

Like the generation immediately before them, the under-18 set has been largely responsible for a dramatic national shift in the concept of mealtime. Part of a snacking and grazing generation, these young chefs and foodies are fans of small bites and mini meals that work perfectly for their on-the-go lifestyles.

In these recipes, you'll find the hallmarks of classic "fun food" but with a decidedly sophisticated twist. The handheld bites in this chapter serve well as party fare, snacks, or even, in some cases, a light repast.

KEY: **GF** Gluten Free   **VG** Vegan   **V** Vegetarian

Gabe Rubin
Portland, Oregon

Six-year-old Gabe Rubin has been working in the garden with his parents since he was a toddler. However, harvesting the family's bounty is not child's play for the Portland youngster, who was eager to get into the kitchen with his parents from the time he could walk. Of all the vegetables that he helps grow, kale—both the more common Lacinato and the purplish Redbor—is his favorite. Although he's only started to use the stove and oven, Gabe has been making kale chips for a couple of years with the use of a dehydrator. The fun part, he says, is experimenting with different flavored chips that he then shares with his family and his classmates. Some of his more interesting combinations have included smoked paprika with cashew and miso sesame, but now he's onto creating flavors for dehydrated tomato chips. After a lot of trial and error, Gabe has found that he likes sweet, sour, and salty combinations best, as in the **Dairy-Free Cheesy Kale Chips**. Because he's interested in animal-free diets, this kale recipe is a favorite. Although it's dairy-free, it has a rich cheese-like flavor from the nutritional yeast.

DAIRY-FREE CHEESY KALE CHIPS

SERVES 4 TO 6

- 1 large bunch lacinato (Tuscan) kale, stems removed
- 3 tablespoons tahini
- 1 tablespoon sesame seeds
  Grated zest and juice of 1 lemon
- 2 teaspoons maple syrup
- 2 teaspoons soy sauce
- ½ teaspoon onion powder
- 2 tablespoons nutritional yeast

1. Preheat the oven to 350°F. Line a baking sheet with parchment paper. (Alternatively, use a food dehydrator; see step 4.)

2. Wash and dry the kale. Tear the kale into chip-size pieces.

3. In a medium bowl, combine the tahini, sesame seeds, lemon zest and juice, maple syrup, soy sauce, onion powder, and nutritional yeast. Whisk to combine. Add the kale and, using your hands, massage the seasoning mixture into the leaves to ensure they are coated evenly.

4. Spread the kale out on the baking sheet and bake until the chips are very crisp but not beginning to brown, 15 to 20 minutes. Turn the chips over halfway through baking if necessary. (Alternatively, set a food dehydrator to 115° to 125°F. Spread the kale on trays and dehydrate for 8 to 12 hours.)

5. Kale chips can be stored in an airtight container for up to 1 week.

Catherine Amoriggi
Warwick, Rhode Island

At age 5, Catherine Amoriggi stood on a kitchen chair to make cavatelli with her dad, offering step-by-step commentary while pretending that she was a cooking show host. At 14, Catherine, who is now a high school junior, started her blog, *Cooking with Cath*, to share the original recipes that had become her consuming passion. That same year she created and hosted an event, cooking and baking for more than 80 people in order to raise money for the Rhode Island Community Food Bank. The young chef earned over $3,000 in donations. That success later encouraged her to use her cooking skills in fundraising efforts for other local organizations like the East Greenwich Animal Protection League.

Eager to continue giving back to the community through her food passion, Catherine spent the summer of 2013 creating a 2014 *365 Food Calendar* to benefit the Rhode Island Community Food Bank. Each month features one of the teen's professionally photographed, original, and seasonal recipes like Bourbon Maple Mousse with a Crisp Topping for November, Champagne Truffles and Decadent Hot Chocolate in February, Spring Roast Herb Chicken, Summer's Harvest Corn and Tomato Spaghetti, and more. Facts about the Rhode Island Community Food Bank and hunger statistics round out the months. To date, over 1,000 of the $15 calendars have been sold, with 100 percent of the proceeds going to the food bank.

"I have been fortunate to grow up in house that always had food. So for me the sad fact that many people—especially kids—don't have an adequate amount of food bothered me so much that I wanted to do something about it," she says.

Catherine uses duck fat to fry her **Pancetta Sweet Pea Fritters** because, compared with regular oil, she says, the duck fat offers a richer, yet not overwhelming taste. Duck fat can be found in most better supermarkets and certainly in gourmet markets, as well as online. The one caveat: Duck fat is expensive. So Catherine suggests you reduce the amount to a third and replace the rest with a flavorless oil like safflower as a way to get the taste without the cost.

(continued)

PANCETTA SWEET PEA FRITTERS

Fritters

- 1 pound shelled fresh peas or thawed frozen peas
- Sea salt
- 1 teaspoon olive oil
- 2 tablespoons minced pancetta
- 1 medium onion, finely minced
- 1/8 teaspoon red pepper flakes
- 1 cup all-purpose flour
- 1/2 teaspoon baking soda
- 1/2 teaspoon baking powder
- 1/8 teaspoon paprika
- 3 eggs, beaten
- 1 teaspoon finely chopped fresh parsley
- Freshly cracked black pepper
- 1/4 cup heavy (whipping) cream
- 5 to 7 cups rendered duck fat (and/or oil), for frying

Dipping sauce

- 1/2 cup crème fraîche or sour cream
- 1/2 cup finely grated Pecorino Romano cheese
- Lemon zest from one lemon (optional)
- Sea salt and freshly cracked black pepper
- 1/4 cup water

1. For the fritters: If you are using fresh peas, bring 4 cups water and 1 teaspoon salt to a boil in a medium saucepan. Have a large bowl of ice water ready. Add the peas to the boiling water and boil for about 1 minute. Drain the peas and immediately add them to the ice water. Drain immediately and set aside.

2. In a skillet, add the olive oil to coat the pan and heat over medium heat. Add the pancetta and cook until all the fat has been rendered out, 5 to 6 minutes. Using a slotted spoon, remove the pancetta from the pan and place it on a plate lined with paper towels.

3. Add the onion to the skillet with the rendered pancetta fat. Add the pepper flakes and a healthy pinch of sea salt. Cook over medium-low heat until the onions are softened and translucent, about 3 minutes. Remove the pan from the heat and set the onions aside to cool.

4. In a large bowl, mix together the flour, baking soda, baking powder, and paprika and whisk so they are well combined. Add the peas and eggs. Stir to combine well and add the cooled onions and pancetta. Add the parsley, 1 teaspoon salt, and black pepper to taste.

5. In a separate bowl, whisk the cream until soft peaks form. Gently fold this into the fritter batter and set aside.

6. In a medium saucepan, heat the duck fat (and/or oil) until a deep-frying thermometer reads about 360°F (or until a pea-size amount of the batter sizzles immediately when dropped into the oil).

7. Drop 1 heaping tablespoon of the fritter batter into the oil. Repeat until enough fritters comfortably fit into the pan without crowding—3 or 4 fritters at a time. Fry the fritters until golden brown, about 3 minutes. Using a slotted spoon, transfer the fritters to a plate lined with paper towels and sprinkle with sea salt. Repeat until all of the fritters are fried.

8. Meanwhile, for the dipping sauce: In a small bowl, mix together the crème fraîche, Pecorino Romano, lemon zest (if using), and sea salt and pepper to taste. Add water and mix well.

9. Serve the fritters hot with the dipping sauce.

Katherine Murphy
Brownsville, Texas

Cataloging the recipes of her great-grandmothers—Florence Murphy and Louise Tiemeyer—for posterity is one of Katherine Murphy's goals. "I have an old cookbook full of handwritten recipes that are unique to my family, and I would love to share them with the world. Their recipes are too good to be kept hidden," says the 17-year-old South Texas blogger.

Summers spent at Grandmother Murphy's North Carolina farm mean cooking and preserving the more-than-enough bounty from the gardens. "My grandmother cooks by experience and feel, but she has infinite patience with me as I measure everything out and recheck a recipe three times," says Katherine, whose blog *The Peanut Butter Lover* features everything from the Mexican and Tex-Mex dishes she knows so well—thanks to her regional upbringing near the border—to new foods she wants to experiment with.

Her **Classic Hummus** recipe came about when fellow food bloggers expressed shock that Katherine had never tried the now-popular Mediterranean snack. After sampling a store-bought version, Katherine says she and her mom "eventually became addicted to nearly every type of hummus out there." Practicality soon spurred creativity and the need to make their own version.

"Because we were consuming an embarrassing amount of hummus, we decided that there had to be a more economically friendly way to handle our obsession," says Katherine. "After a few trial runs and adding and removing some ingredients here and there, I managed to create a hummus recipe that has become our go-to. It's incredibly easy."

CLASSIC HUMMUS
SERVES 4

1 cup cooked chickpeas
½ cup tahini
3 cloves garlic, peeled
Juice of 2 lemons
Salt and freshly ground black pepper
1 tablespoon olive oil
1 tablespoon finely chopped fresh parsley
½ teaspoon paprika
Pita bread or Homemade Pita Chips (recipe follows), for serving

1. In a blender or food processor, combine the chickpeas, tahini, garlic, lemon juice, 3 tablespoons water, and salt and pepper to taste. Process until smooth, adding more water as needed to achieve a thick smooth paste that is easily spreadable.

2. Spoon the mixture into a shallow dish. Make a depression in the middle and pour the olive oil into it. Garnish with parsley and paprika. Serve with pita bread or pita chips.

Homemade Pita Chips

Pita chips are now as ubiquitous and commercially available as potato and tortilla chips, but they are relatively easy to make at home. You can experiment with both white and whole wheat pitas when making chips, as well as a variety of seasonings to suit your taste. Homemade pita chips are best stored in an airtight container or a zip-top bag for up to 1 week.

3 large pita breads, plain or whole wheat
½ cup extra virgin olive oil
Coarse salt
Sesame seeds, black pepper, garlic powder, oregano, or sumac (optional)

1. Preheat the oven to 400°F.

2. Slice each pita bread into 8 to 10 wedges. Brush each wedge with olive oil and place on a baking sheet. Season the pita chips with coarse salt to taste. Sprinkle with sesame seeds or any combination of the optional spices to taste.

3. Bake until the pita chips are golden brown and crusty, about 10 minutes.

4. Remove from the oven and cool completely before serving.

Avery McNew
Niles, Michigan

Taking a cue from her animal friends is often how vegan 10-year-old Avery McNew gets her ideas for new dishes. Greens like clover or sorrel that her family's horses seem to enjoy might make their way into her human family's dinnertime salad. And it was her Apple Oat Balls, originally created as a treat for the equines after horse shows, but equally delicious for humans, that got Avery invited to the White House as a winner of the First Lady's Healthy Lunchtime Challenge in 2013.

"I want to help people change the *way* they see food," she says. "There is a social norm that we need to eat meat at the dinner table. I'd like to help kids and parents understand *who* they were eating, so they know *what* they are eating in the future."

Next to helping animals, Avery's main goal when she cooks is to not actually cook at all. Her recipes tend to feature raw ingredients. This **Edamame Hummus** came about because Avery doesn't particularly care for the traditional kind of hummus—and edamame are a staple in her home.

Beyond her personal directive to eat harm-free food, when it comes to cooking, Avery's main credo is that there are no rules. "Food can even be artistic! There are infinite possibilities and you can experiment," she says. "But most of all, your food choices can make you healthier and express your beliefs at the same time."

EDAMAME HUMMUS
SERVES 4 TO 6

2 cups shelled edamame, cooked
1 to 2 cloves garlic, peeled
½ (12-ounce) block silken tofu, drained
½ cup lemon juice
¼ cup extra virgin olive oil
1 teaspoon ground cumin
¾ teaspoon coarse salt
Fresh cilantro and/or fresh flat-leaf parsley, for garnish
Toasted naan bread, pita chips, carrots, or celery, for dipping

1. In a food processor, the edamame, garlic, tofu, lemon juice, olive oil, cumin, and salt and process until smooth, 1 to 2 minutes.

2. Transfer to a serving bowl and garnish with cilantro and/or parsley. Serve with naan, pita chips, carrots, or celery for dipping.

Kenny Seals-Nutt
Charlotte, North Carolina

Art alongside industry is the way honors student Kenny Seals-Nutt approaches cooking. The young man first got into the kitchen to bake cookies, which his mom sold at her office as a way for the youngster to earn money for video games. A senior at Hickory Grove Christian School, Kenny credits his faith with all that came next, including the chance to earn money for college with his own catering business at 14 and the opportunity to work as a pasta chef at an Italian restaurant in his hometown of Charlotte beginning when he was 16. Working at the restaurant, he says, with others who watched his every move, helped him gain confidence in his craft as well as overcome what he calls his "innate shyness."

"The experience taught me to handle rejection and constructive criticism, which then made me more appreciative when someone complimented my work." He also volunteers making meals for the local chapter of the Ronald McDonald House, which provides a home environment for children undergoing treatment for serious illness at local hospitals. Kenny's short-term dream includes attending both an Ivy League school and the Culinary Institute of America, but he plans to be the White House chef in the long-term. He doesn't see a serious academic career and a culinary career as incompatible because, he says, all of his dishes represent more than something to eat. They represent culture, history, math, science, and more.

"What makes this industry so special to me is that it is one of the few activities that let me utilize everything I love to do. The accelerated mathematics I take at school lets me analyze the statistics and operations of my catering business. I have a keen appreciation for science, and cooking allows me to see the chemical reactions that make certain dishes delicious," he says. "I also love the arts, and there is no more expressive and personal art form than cooking, which can unify cultures just like music, literature, and cinema do."

Kenny's **Crab-Stuffed Tempura Jalapeños with Mango Chutney Dipping Sauce** is an evolution of a format that he finds himself experimenting with over and over: more sophisticated versions of classic deep-fried snacks. Better quality ingredients are the hallmark of his small bites. Kenny's versions can feature anything from Philly cheesesteak and Sriracha to the crab and pancetta in these stuffed jalapeños.

(continued)

CRAB-STUFFED TEMPURA JALAPEÑOS WITH MANGO CHUTNEY DIPPING SAUCE

SERVES 4 TO 6

Chutney dipping sauce

2 tablespoons olive oil

1 red onion, finely diced

1 clove garlic, minced

2 inches fresh ginger, peeled and minced

½ cup packed light brown sugar

⅓ cup apple cider vinegar

¼ cup orange juice

1 cup tamarind juice or nectar

5 fresh mangoes, diced, or 5 cups frozen, diced mango

¼ cup dried cranberries or raisins

Pinch of curry powder (optional)

Jalapeños and filling

15 large jalapeño peppers

⅓ cup finely chopped smoked pancetta

1 shallot, minced

3 tablespoons white wine

1 cup lump crabmeat

5 cloves garlic, minced

1 teaspoon Worcestershire sauce

Juice of ½ lemon

2 tablespoons finely chopped fresh parsley

2 ounces cream cheese

Salt and freshly ground black pepper

Tempura batter

1 egg, chilled

1 cup ice water

1 cup all-purpose flour, sifted

1 teaspoon Spanish paprika

¼ teaspoon baking soda

2 quarts vegetable oil, for deep-frying

½ lemon, for serving

1. For the dipping sauce: In a medium saucepan, heat the olive oil over medium-high heat. Add the onion, garlic, and ginger and cook until just softened, about 1 minute. Add the brown sugar, vinegar, orange juice, and tamarind juice, and bring the mixture to a boil, stirring until the sugar is completely dissolved. Add the mangoes, cranberries or raisins, and curry powder (if using) and reduce the heat to low. Simmer for about 2 hours to thicken the chutney to the consistency of a loose preserve. Set aside to cool.

2. For the jalapeños and filling: Halve each jalapeño lengthwise and, using a paring knife, carefully scrape out all seeds and membranes. Set aside.

3. Place the pancetta in a medium skillet while the pan is still cold, then place it over medium heat and cook for about 1 minute. Add the shallot and cook until the shallot becomes translucent, 1 to 2 minutes. Add the wine and simmer for 1 minute. Add the crabmeat, garlic, Worcestershire sauce, and lemon juice. Heat until the crabmeat is just warmed, about 2 minutes.

4. Transfer the crab mixture to a medium bowl. Add the parsley and cream cheese and carefully stir until combined, but without breaking the crabmeat. Season with salt and black pepper to taste.

5. Divide the crab mixture evenly among the 30 jalapeño halves. Be sure that the mixture is packed tightly in the peppers. Refrigerate for 30 minutes to 1 hour or until they are completely cold.

6. Meanwhile, for the tempura batter: In a medium bowl, whisk the egg while gradually pouring in the ice water. In another medium bowl, whisk together the flour, paprika, and baking soda. Gradually add the flour mixture to the egg mixture, stirring the ingredients together gently until they combine. Do not overmix. Refrigerate for 20 minutes.

7. In a large, deep skillet, heat 2 to 3 inches of oil over medium heat until a deep-frying thermometer reads 350°F (or until a pinch of flour dropped into the oil sizzles).

8. Remove the jalapeños and the batter from the refrigerator. Using cooking tongs, dip the jalapeños, one at a time, into the tempura batter, turning until evenly coated and then placing directly in the hot oil. Be sure not to crowd the jalapeños in the skillet. Cook until the peppers are golden brown on all sides, 2 to 3 minutes. Remove the jalapeños and place on a plate lined with paper towel or on a wire rack set over a rimmed baking sheet. Repeat until all the jalapeños are cooked, adding and heating more oil as necessary.

9. Lightly squeeze the lemon over the cooked jalapeños. Serve hot with chutney dipping sauce.

Justin G. Goodwin
Far Rockaway, New York

Living in Queens, New York, the most diverse ethnic community in America, has heightened Justin Goodwin's interest in international foods like Thai, Mexican, and authentic Italian. He counts his mother's gift of a KitchenAid stand mixer and some extra attachments when he was 11 years old as a turning point in his culinary life. Interested in joining his mother in the kitchen from the time he was in third grade, the 13-year-old, who attends P.S. 114 in Far Rockaway, Queens, volunteers time cooking for the needy at the Alive Ministry church shelter and at the local community garden—when he's not on the football field or drawing cartoons. Securing a place at Manhattan's Food and Finance High School is one of Justin's priorities, after which he plans to attend culinary school in Paris. For now, though, his main goal is taking over some of the home cooking so his single mom doesn't have to cook all the family meals alone. This meal—**Shredded Pork Tacos with Pineapple Salsa**—is easy to put together on a busy school night as long as you get the pork going in the slow cooker in the morning.

SHREDDED PORK TACOS WITH PINEAPPLE SALSA

Shredded pork

1 tablespoon ground cumin

2 teaspoons ground black pepper

2 teaspoons chili powder

1 teaspoon dried oregano

1 teaspoon paprika

1 teaspoon salt

½ teaspoon red pepper flakes

½ teaspoon onion powder

2 cloves garlic, smashed to a paste

2 to 3 pounds boneless pork shoulder

Pineapple salsa

1⅓ cups chopped fresh pineapple

½ large red bell pepper, chopped

1 small chile pepper, minced

½ medium red onion, chopped

¼ cup chopped fresh cilantro

Juice of ½ lime

Salt

Tacos

16 to 18 soft taco shells

2 cups shredded Monterey jack cheese

6 ounces sour cream

1 avocado, thinly sliced

1. For the shredded pork: In a small bowl, mix together the cumin, black pepper, chili powder, oregano, paprika, salt, pepper flakes, onion powder, and garlic to create a grainy paste. Rub this paste all over the pork shoulder and place it in an electric slow cooker and cook on low for 6 to 8 hours or until able to shred the meat with a fork. (Alternatively, place the pork shoulder in a baking dish and cover with foil. Bake at 250°F for about 7 hours, or until you are able to shred the meat easily with a fork.)

2. Meanwhile, for the salsa: In a medium bowl, mix together the pineapple, bell pepper, chile, onion, cilantro, and lime juice. Add salt to taste and set aside.

3. For the tacos: When the pork is cooked, shred using a fork. Place 2 or 3 table-spoons of shredded pork on a taco shell and sprinkle with the Monterey jack, about 2 teaspoons sour cream, some pineapple salsa, and a thin slice of avocado. Repeat until all the tacos are made.

Haile Thomas
Tucson, Arizona

Haile Thomas has been the First Lady's guest at a State of the Union address, was a guest star on a Food Network series, is a part of the advisory board of a major food magazine, and has created a charity that enables kids to be healthier through cooking classes and exercise regimens. She does all this between consulting for Hyatt hotels alongside luminary chef Alice Waters on the hotel chain's kids' menu, starring in her own YouTube series, and attending seventh grade. As much of a culinary prodigy as 13-year-old Haile may be, she credits the influence of her Jamaican-immigrant parents for her love of food and her outgoing personality. Haile's signature dish, **Curried Shrimp Lettuce Wraps,** is an evolution of a Jamaican favorite that she adapted when her father was diagnosed with diabetes in 2009. "Traditionally curry shrimp is served with white rice and a rich sauce, which is very delicious but a little heavy," she says. "After testing out different ways to prepare this dish, I found that it was super fun to eat out of lettuce cups and even yummier lightened up with fresh veggies and herbs in a lighter curry sauce."

(continued)

CURRIED SHRIMP
LETTUCE WRAPS

Seasoning mix

1 teaspoon ground coriander

1 teaspoon ground cumin

1 teaspoon Jamaican curry powder

1 teaspoon paprika

1 teaspoon lemon-pepper seasoning

Shrimp

1 pound tiger shrimp, peeled, deveined, and chopped into medium pieces

3 tablespoons grapeseed oil

1 medium red onion, thinly sliced

1 red bell pepper, finely chopped

1 yellow bell pepper, finely chopped

3 cloves garlic, minced

1 pint cherry tomatoes, halved

2 scallions, thinly sliced

1 handful fresh cilantro, chopped

Juice of 1 lemon

2 Hass avocados, sliced

8 butter lettuce leaves

1. For the seasoning mix: In a medium bowl, combine the coriander, cumin, curry powder, paprika, and lemon pepper and whisk well.

2. For the shrimp: Add the shrimp to the seasoning mix and toss together. Place in the refrigerator to marinate for 15 minutes.

3. In a medium skillet, heat the grapeseed oil over medium-high heat. Add the onion and bell peppers and cook, stirring occasionally, until the onion and pepper begin to soften, about 3 minutes. Stir in the garlic and cook 1 minute more.

4. Add the seasoned shrimp and cook until the shrimp pieces just begin to turn pink, 3 to 4 minutes. Stir in the tomatoes, scallions, and cilantro and let cook until the tomatoes begin to soften, 1 more minute. Remove the pan from the heat.

5. Pour the lemon juice on top of the avocado slices.

6. Lay the lettuce leaves out on a clean work surface and spoon about 1 heaping tablespoon of the shrimp mixture down the center of each lettuce leaf. Layer with one or two slices of avocado, or more if you prefer. Fold the leaf up and over the filling and arrange on a platter.

Logan Bello
Sebastopol, California

It was a savvy fourth grade teacher who first realized that Logan Bello needed a creative outlet to channel his love of food. "I was constantly talking about cooking in class, so my teacher, Mrs. Amador, suggested I start journaling my food adventures," says Logan. "It evolved into the food blog *Logans Bites*."

A World War II history buff, Logan also has an insatiable hunger for international food culture, which he ascribes to traveling with his parents and their willingness to allow him and his sister to order off the adult menu in fine restaurants, regardless of exotic locale, from the time they were 5 years old. Now 13, Logan says he has a particular passion for Hawaiian food specifically because of the mix of cultures it represents including Native Hawaiian, Asian, Portuguese, and Japanese. He is also deeply intersted in the Asian-influenced flavors within his mother's Dutch heritage, such as those from Indonesia.

Yet, as devoted as he is to cooking, the eighth grader isn't so sure he wants to open a restaurant himself one day. "Through my food adventures, I've fallen in love with a handful of really great restaurants and then watched them fall apart after about a year or so. It breaks my heart, so I know that being a great chef is really competitive and a lot of hard work," he says. "Whatever I do wind up doing, I have the appreciation for really great food, the knowledge of where food comes from, and the awareness of the difference in quality of ingredients and tastes."

Logan taught himself to make *shumai,* Japanese dumplings, because it is one his favorite Asian restaurant dishes, rife with Far East flavor profiles including ginger, soy, and sesame oil. Use ponzu sauce or simple soy sauce for dipping his **Pork & Mushroom Shumai.**

(continued)

PORK & MUSHROOM SHUMAI

SERVES 4 TO 6

1¼ pounds ground pork

½ cup chopped cremini mushrooms

1 clove garlic, chopped

1 tablespoon chopped fresh ginger

2 tablespoons chopped scallions

1 tablespoon soy sauce

1 tablespoon toasted sesame oil

Freshly ground black pepper

1 package round wrappers (for dumplings or potstickers)

1 egg, beaten

Cooking spray

Soy sauce or ponzu sauce, for serving

1. In a food processor, combine ground pork, mushrooms, garlic, ginger, and scallions and pulse a few times to mix the ingredients. Add the soy sauce, sesame oil, and pepper to taste. Pulse until all the ingredients are well incorporated.

2. Remove the wrappers from package. Make an A-OK sign with your nondominant hand by creating a circle with your thumb and pointing finger. Place a wrapper on top of the circle between your thumb and forefinger.

3. Brush the wrapper lightly with the beaten egg and then place 1 tablespoon of the pork and mushroom mixture into the center of the wrapper. Gently push the filling down into the indentation and then bring the edges of the wrapper inward, until it is almost but not completely closed. The shumai will look like a small, slightly open bag. Repeat this step, filling egg roll wrappers, until all of the filling is used up.

4. Line a bamboo steamer or metal steamer insert with a sheet of wax paper cut to fit. If you are using stackable steamer baskets, line each one in this manner and coat the paper lightly with cooking spray.

5. Place the dumplings into the baskets, being careful not to crowd them. There should be at least ¼ inch of space around each shumai. Place the steamer over a wok or saucepan of boiling water. The water should reach just below the base of the first basket. Cover and steam for 7 to 8 minutes. Carefully remove the dumplings and serve with soy or ponzu sauce.

Daiquiri Przybyla
Penacook, New Hampshire

Eighteen-year-old Daiquiri Przybyla has many goals. In addition to opening her own restaurant one day, she plans to complete associate's degrees in baking and culinary arts and then masters and doctoral degrees in food science. These are not small goals, especially, Daiquiri acknowledges, for a girl with a past like hers.

"My life wasn't as good as I wanted it to be," she says of the days when, as a 14-year-old, she became a heavy drinker and regularly smoked marijuana, often bringing liquor she pinched from her father's stash to sell at school. A physically abusive home life led her to stray further, becoming pregnant at 16 and giving birth in the middle of her senior year to her daughter, Ally, who is now almost 2 years old.

Bewildered, abandoned by friends, and pushed out of her parents' home, Daiquiri was scrambling for a lifeline. She found it in the culinary classes she had begun in her junior year. An avid home cook who cooked alongside her mother and grandmother, Daiquiri found a safe haven in the exploration and creative opportunities of the formal cooking program.

"It was the push of having to provide for someone else that made me realize I had to fight through the stray, careless life I had been living," she says. After the birth of her daughter, she enrolled in a local community college culinary program while at the same time raising her child alone and trying to complete the requirements of her senior year, finally graduating in 2013. She hopes her future culinary adventures—both hands-on and academic—will help her change lives the way hers has been changed—particularly in parts of the world where hunger and malnutrition are issues.

The young cook's signature dish is the **Mushroom & Onion Pierogies** she learned how to make from her grandmother. Making them is a way, she says, to remind herself where she comes from. While she is estranged from her family, preparing this comfort food doesn't make her sad or angry, says Daiquiri, instead the pierogies serve as a link to a larger cultural heritage that she hopes to share with her daughter one day, as a tangible way to anchor their place in the world. While the recipe comes from the Polish side of her background, she's been known to serve them with an Italian sauce or an Irish cabbage that represent other aspects of her ethnicity.

MUSHROOM & ONION PIEROGIES

Beet sauce

1 medium beet

1 teaspoon extra virgin olive oil

½ teaspoon sea salt

2 teaspoons canola or other vegetable oil

1 carrot, finely diced

1 stalk celery, finely diced

1 onion, finely diced

1 tablespoon cornstarch dissolved in
   1 tablespoon cold water

¼ teaspoon salt

¼ teaspoon white pepper

Pierogies

3 tablespoons canola or other vegetable
   oil

8 ounces white mushrooms, finely diced

1 medium onion, finely diced

½ teaspoon salt

¼ teaspoon white pepper

2 cups all-purpose flour

½ cup hot water

¼ cup cold water

6 tablespoons butter

1. For the beet sauce: Preheat the oven to 400°F. Wash the beet and place on a large square of foil. Drizzle the beet with the olive oil and sprinkle with the sea salt. Wrap the foil around the beet and place it in a baking dish. Bake until the beet is fork-tender, 30 to 40 minutes. Remove from the oven and allow to cool completely. When the beet is cool enough to handle, peel.

2. In a medium saucepan, bring 2 cups water to a boil. Add the roasted beet and simmer until the beet is very soft, about 15 minutes. Reserving the broth, remove the beet from the water. When the beet is cool enough to handle, grate using a box grater.

3. In a medium skillet, heat the canola oil over medium heat. Add the carrot, celery, and onion and cook until the onion begins to soften and release aromas, 3 to 4 minutes. Add the shredded beet and cook for 1 minute more. Add the reserved beet broth and simmer the mixture for 10 minutes.

4. Use a slotted spoon to strain out and discard the vegetables from the broth. Return the broth to a simmer once again. Add the

(continued)

cornstarch mixture to the broth, increase the heat to high and bring it to a boil. When the mixture comes to a boil, reduce once again to a simmer until it thickens enough to coat the back of a spoon evenly, 1 to 2 minutes. Add salt and pepper. Set the beet sauce aside. It can be served either warm or at room temperature.

5. For the pierogies: Heat a large skillet over medium heat and add 2 tablespoons of the canola oil. Add the mushrooms and onion and cook until the onion is tender and translucent, 4 to 5 minutes. Season with the salt and white pepper and mix well. Remove from heat and set the filling aside to cool.

6. In a medium bowl, combine the flour and $\frac{1}{4}$ cup of the hot water. Mix well and cover with a moist towel. Allow to rest for 10 minutes, then add $\frac{1}{4}$ cup cold water and knead it into the dough. Cover the dough and allow to rest again for 15 minutes. Add the remaining $\frac{1}{4}$ cup hot water and the remaining 1 tablespoon canola oil. Mix and knead the dough well for about 5 minutes, or until

smooth and elastic. It will be slightly gummy to the touch. Cover with a damp cloth and set it aside to rest for 15 more minutes.

7. After the dough has rested, divide it into three equal pieces. Roll out one piece of dough to an $\frac{1}{8}$-inch thickness. Using a 3-inch round cookie or biscuit cutter, cut the dough into rounds. Repeat with the remaining two pieces of dough and cut out more rounds.

8. Hold a dough round in your hand and place 1 teaspoon of the filling in the middle and fold it in half, as you would a taco, then pinch the edges tightly closed while lightly pulling and stretching them. Fill and fold all the dough rounds.

9. In a medium skillet, melt the butter over medium-low heat. Add 3 or 4 pierogies to the pan. Do not overcrowd them. Allow the pierogies to brown lightly on one side, about 3 minutes, then gently flip the pierogies to brown on the other side, about 3 minutes more. Repeat with the remaining pierogies. Serve drizzled with the beet sauce.

Mason Partak
Auburn, California

After winning the $35 prize at a local cookie-baking contest when he was 7 years old, Mason Partak discovered the competition bug had bitten him. Following in the footsteps of his mom, Kathy, who is an avid recipe contestant and cooking demonstrator, Mason branched out on his own during his town's TomatoFest where the success of his presentation led to invitations to demonstrate recipes at the Strawberry Festival, the Spring Auburn Home Show, the California State Fair, and the Sonoma County Fair as well as to make television appearances in New York.

Now 10 years old, he is currently turning his skills toward raising funds to buy a stove and oven for Alta Vista Community Charter School where he is a fourth grader. The appliances would not only support a culinary program, but also allow hot, fresh lunches to be cooked onsite.

"I know if other kids my age can learn to cook, their self confidence will go up like mine has," says Mason, who raised nearly $6,000 toward his goal within a few months' time.

His signature **Beef Sliders** recipe is a result of a contest run by Snow's Citrus Court, a citrus grower and product manufacturer in nearby Newcastle, California. "I won second place in the main dish category and it won the Snow's Citrus Court Award, a $50 award for the best use of a Snow's product," says Mason of his mini-burgers, which are flavored with a Mandarin orange jam that provides a sweet and sour tang to balance the meaty juiciness of the beef and bacon. The sliders feature just a little kick from red pepper flakes, but you may reduce or increase the amount according to your taste.

Making Any Pan Nonstick

Any pan can be "nonstick" if you know how to use it. When browning proteins like chicken breasts, chops, steaks, or burgers, heat your skillet over medium heat. Then add oil or cooking spray if your recipe calls for it. Once you place your protein in the plan, *leave it alone!* The time will vary depending on the protein, but generally 7 to 8 minutes per side for a chicken breast and 10 to 12 minutes for steak. You may test whether the protein is ready to be flipped by gently lifting a corner and seeing if it sticks. Once it is browned, it will "release" itself from the pan and flip easily. Follow the cooking time instructions based on your particular cut of meat to ensure that the item is well browned.

BEEF SLIDERS

Sliders

1 pound lean ground beef

1 egg

¼ cup finely minced peel of a fresh mandarin orange or tangerine

1 cup crushed saltine crackers

½ cup Mandarin orange fruit spread or tangerine marmalade

2 scallions, minced

¼ small red onion, minced

½ teaspoon seasoning salt

½ teaspoon red pepper flakes

¼ cup warm water

1 ounce dry onion soup mix or green onion (scallion) dip mix

½ cup chopped cooked bacon

Cooking spray

Sauce

2 tablespoons Mandarin orange fruit spread or tangerine marmalade

2 tablespoons hot pepper sauce or Chinese hot mustard (or less to taste)

Assembly

8 slider rolls

Thinly sliced red onion

Thinly sliced tomato

Shredded iceberg lettuce

1. For the sliders: In a large bowl, combine all the ingredients except cooking spray and knead well with your hands until all the ingredients are well mixed. Form the meat mixture into 8 small patties, about 3 inches in diameter.

2. Heat a large skillet over medium heat and coat with cooking spray. Add the sliders, being sure not to crowd them in the pan. Cook until nicely browned, 5 to 6 minutes on each side.

3. Meanwhile, for the sauce: In a small bowl, mixing together the marmalade and hot sauce (or mustard).

4. To assemble the sliders: Place a slider on a roll, drizzle with about 1 teaspoon sauce, and garnish as desired with onion, tomato, and lettuce.

Nikita Bhuyan
Phoenix, Arizona

When she's not practicing her ten-year passion for Indian classical, Bollywood, fusion, and folk dances from various Indian states, including her original Assam, Nikita Bhuyan serves on the Wellness Committee for the Tempe Union High School District where she is a junior at Desert Vista High. While the teen is proud to sit on a committee with administrators, teachers, and local health organizations, she is most proud of managing the club she started to educate other teens about nutrition and cooking. "Our club takes regular recipes and then creates healthier versions of them," says Nikita, who regularly appears on local news shows to do cooking demonstrations. It's the beginning of what she hopes will be a lifelong career working with young people in the field of nutrition. For now, Nikita shares her message with a larger audience through both a Facebook page and her own blog, *Nikita's Tasty and Healthy Dishes*.

The bright flavors of Mediterranean cuisine are a favorite of Nikita's and she created her **Mini Mediterranean Calzones** as a way of melding some of those that she most likes. She particularly notes the pleasing contrast of sweet from the bell peppers and salt from the cheese. While creating the dish, she says she kept in mind that the recipe should be easy to cook and healthy, as a way to encourage both other people her age, as well as adults, to move toward better food choices.

MINI MEDITERRANEAN CALZONES

MAKES 10 MINI CALZONES

1 red bell pepper, halved

Cooking spray

6 to 8 ounces boneless, skinless chicken breast

Salt and freshly ground black pepper

1 package (16 ounces) ready-made pizza dough (or the dough in the Cornmeal Pizza Dough Parmesan Crisps, page 184)

6 generous tablespoons hummus, store-bought or homemade (Classic Hummus, page 38)

2 scant tablespoons pesto, store-bought or homemade (Superhero Pesto, page 75)

6 generous tablespoons crumbled reduced-fat feta cheese

1 egg, beaten (optional)

1. Preheat an outdoor grill or stovetop grill pan to high. Lightly coat the pepper with cooking spray. Place the pepper skin-side down on the grill and cook until the pepper begins to blister, 3 to 5 minutes. Turn the pepper halves over and cook 3 minutes more. (Alternatively, heat a medium skillet over medium heat and coat the pan lightly with cooking spray. Slice the pepper into small chunks and add them to the pan. Sauté on medium until the pepper slices begin to char and blister, 5 to 7 minutes.) Remove from the heat and set aside to cool. Cut into pieces.

2. Season the chicken with salt and pepper. Place on the heated grill and cook for 7 to 8 minutes, flip over and cook until the chicken breast is seared and completely cooked through, 7 to 8 minutes more. (Alternatively, heat a medium skillet over medium heat. Coat the pan lightly with cooking spray and add the chicken breast. Cook over medium heat for 7 to 8 minutes per side or until the breast is lightly browned and cooked completely through.) Let the chicken rest for 5 minutes, then cut into small chunks. Set aside.

3. Preheat the oven to 350°F. Lightly coat a baking sheet with cooking spray or line with parchment paper.

4. Divide the pizza dough into 10 equal balls, each about the size of a golf ball. Flatten a ball with your palm into a disk and continue to flatten and pull gently into a round that is about 6 inches wide. Spread 2 teaspoons hummus in the middle of the dough round, followed by ½ teaspoon pesto, and 2 or 3 pieces each of grilled pepper and chicken. Top with 2 teaspoons feta. Fold the dough over and crimp the edges of the calzone with a fork to ensure that there are no openings for the fillings to ooze out while baking. Repeat for all the dough portions to make 10 mini calzones.

5. If desired, brush the calzones with beaten egg for a shiny golden top. Arrange the finished calzones on the baking sheet and bake until golden brown, 25 to 30 minutes. Serve hot.

From the Street Corner to the Kitchen

Steven Amoros

Bronx, New York

From his home in Puerto Rico to a homeless shelter in Rockaway, New York, to running with what he calls a "bad group" in the South Bronx where his family eventually settled, 17-year-old Steven Amoros has taken the long way to the kitchen. By the time he was in his second year of high school, Steven's grade point average plummeted. He was, he says, also well on his way to following in the footsteps of his older brother who had been arrested and served repeated jail sentences for robbery.

"My mom wanted me to leave school and work, to find a different path," says Steven. "I knew I had to make a change. The worst part is that I was valedictorian of my fifth grade class. I'm not a dumb kid." Help came from his older sister who suggested Steven follow her footsteps and attend a charter high school for kids in danger of dropping out of school. Focused on mixing academics with internships geared toward job-development skills, John V. Lindsay Wildcat Academy is known for its culinary program and hydroponic garden initiative created in concert with Steven Ritz's Bronx Green Machine aquaponics program. Culinary- and farming-focused programs such as these, popping up around the country, aim to reach and empower at-risk kids through the universality of food.

The culinary program at Wildcat was particularly appealing to Steven because even as a little boy he found himself mesmerized by the goings-on in the family kitchen where his mother and sisters cooked traditional Puerto Rican dishes like pasteles, a Christmas favorite. Pasteles are meat-based turnovers that most closely resemble Mexican tamales. The Puerto Rican version uses a mixture of shredded root vegetables as the "dough," versus the corn flour used in Mexican versions.

At Wildcat Academy, the teen, whose home and school are in a neighborhood that comprises a food desert in the poorest congressional district in America, became fascinated with the hydroponic garden that provides fresh food for the students' onsite restaurant and catering facilities.

"Getting into the culinary program opened my eyes and taste buds. It opened me up to different styles of cooking and all the different ways and flavors to do one thing—like creating a vegetarian version of my pasteles for the school restaurant," says Steven.

Pasteles are most commonly made with pork or chicken, so Steven's **Vegetarian Pasteles** version that uses a chickpea filling is a creative and healthy departure from tradition.

Steven has volunteered to talk about the cooking program and hydroponic gardens at events around the city and has been part of public service commercials that have appeared on TNT and Disney channels. "Being able to do those things made me realize I could be someone important. I could help someone else out," says Steven, who volunteers to cook holiday meals for the HELP Morris shelter for families because, he says, his family was once in the same situation.

Besides hoping to eventually get a scholarship to a 4-year college where he can have what he describes as a "real college experience" and study computer science, Steven plans to be valedictorian of his high school class. He studies between cooking meals to aid his ailing mother and working as many stipend hours as he can at the school restaurant in order to supplement the family's food stamps with his earnings. "I work as much as I can, so I can get paid the maximum amount of money. I try not to let anything get past me so I can look out for my mom," he says. "As soon as I finish college and get a good job, priority number one is to get my family out of the 'hood."

The dough in Steven's pasteles is made with starchy yautía (a common Caribbean root vegetable), calabaza (a Caribbean pumpkin), and green bananas to form a thick "meal" that looks similar to moist, grated coconut. Don't be afraid to mold this forgiving dough around the chickpea stuffing as needed and prepare to be surprised when the grated mixture cooks up to a smooth, cohesive casing for the herbaceous and spicy filling—very similar to a Mexican tamale.

The flavor of the banana leaves can be quite overpowering; to counteract this you may want to parboil the leaf squares in lightly salted water for 30 to 40 seconds and then drain and dry them before using them to enfold the *pasteles*.

Yautía

In much of the tropical world, including the Caribbean, Central and South Americas, and Africa, a wide variety of root vegetables serve not just as side dishes but as mainstays in everything from baked goods to stews and even breakfast foods. Yautía, used in Steven Amoros's pastele recipe, tastes somewhat nutty and is extremely starchy and even sticky when raw; when cooked yautía becomes smooth and doughy. Also called cocoyam, malanga, and tannia, yautía belongs to the taro family. It is easily found in Caribbean, African, and Latino markets and should be stored in a cool dry place as you would potatoes.

Vegetarian Pasteles

VG
GF

Stuffing

- 1 tablespoon olive oil
- 1 small onion, chopped
- 4 cloves garlic, minced
- 4 ají dulce chiles, seeded and chopped
- 2 tablespoons Racaito (recipe follows)
- 1 tablespoon Adobo Seasoning (recipe follows)
- 1 tablespoon dried oregano
- 1½ cups cooked chickpeas or 1 can (15 ounces) chickpeas, rinsed and drained
- 1 cup whole green olives, pitted and chopped
- 1 bay leaf

Dough

- ¼ cup canola or other vegetable oil
- 1 tablespoon achiote (annatto) seeds
- 2½ pounds yautía, peeled and finely grated
- 3 green bananas, peeled and finely grated
- ½ pound calabaza, peeled, seeded, and finely grated

Assembly

- 20 parchment paper rectangles (12 × 8-inch)
- 20 banana leaves, cut into 10 × 5-inch rectangles
- 20 lengths (18-inch) kitchen string
- 1 tablespoon coarse salt

1. For the stuffing: In a large skillet, heat the olive oil over medium heat. Add the onion and cook until the onion begins to soften, 1 to 2 minutes. Add the garlic and stir well. Cook for 1 minute more. Add the ají dulce chiles and cook until the peppers begin to soften, 1 to 2 minutes. Add the racaito, adobo seasoning, and oregano and mix well.

2. Place the chickpeas in a food processor and pulse to form a rough meal, about 1 minute. Do not overprocess into a paste.

3. Add this chickpea meal to the onion-pepper mixture along with the olives. Mix very well and add 1 cup water and stir very well. Add the bay leaf. Reduce the heat to a simmer and cook until all the water is reduced, but the mixture is not totally dry, about 8 minutes.

4. For the dough: In a small skillet, heat the oil over medium heat. Add the achiote and cook until the seeds release all of their color and begin to brown. Reserving the oil, strain out and discard the seeds.

5. In a large bowl, mix together the grated yautía, green bananas, and calabaza. Mix very well. Add just enough of the achiote oil to bring the dough together into a firm ball.

6. To assemble the pasteles: Place a parchment sheet on a flat work surface with a long side facing you. Place a banana leaf on top, also with a long side facing you. Place a drop of the remaining achiote oil

(continued)

onto the center of the right half of the banana leaf and place 2 tablespoons of the dough on top of it. Dampen your hands and flatten the dough ball, pressing it out on one half of the leaf, taking it to the edges (but do not let the dough ooze over the edges) to form a rectangle roughly 4 inches tall by 3 inches wide and about ⅛ inch thick.

7. On the other half of the same leaf, make a second dough rectangle right next to the first one, with another drop of achiote oil.

8. Place 1 heaping tablespoon of the stuffing into the center of the first rectangle of dough. Lift up the side of the leaf with the unfilled dough and use it to guide the plain dough on top of the filled dough. Release the leaf and gently press the edges of the two dough rectangles together. Then, using your hands or a rubber spatula, press and mold the filled pastele into a smooth rectangle, like a tamale.

9. Fold the banana leaf over the pastele. Turn the parchment so that a short side is facing you. Place the wrapped pastele at the bottom of the parchment with some room to spare and fold the pastele forward with the parchment one time. Fold the sides of the parchment in toward the pastele and then continue rolling so that it is sealed tightly (like rolling a burrito). Use the kitchen twine to tie the "package" closed. Repeat this technique until all the pasteles are filled, wrapped, and tied in parchment.

10. To cook the pasteles, in a large deep pot, bring 8 cups of water and 1 tablespoon coarse salt to a boil. Add the pasteles gently to the water. Do not overcrowd. Reduce the heat to a simmer and cook for 1½ hours. Remove from pot and carefully unwrap. Serve hot. Cooked pasteles may be frozen in a zip-top bag for up to 2 months.

Recaito

Recaito may be used as a seasoning in soups, stews, or to marinate meats.

- 3 to 4 cubanelle peppers, stemmed and roughly chopped
- 2 medium onions, peeled and halved
- 1 bunch fresh culantro leaves (or 1 cup cilantro leaves)
- 6 ají dulces chiles, stemmed

In a food processor, combine all the ingredients and pulse to a smooth paste. Store refrigerated in an airtight jar.

Adobo Seasoning

Once used as a dry preservative for meats, the advent of the refrigerated age has made adobo a flavor enhancer above all. Turmeric gives adobo the yellow color most associated with Latino Caribbean versions of the mix.

- 6 tablespoons salt
- 6 tablespoons garlic powder
- 4 tablespoons dried oregano
- 2 tablespoons ground black pepper
- 2 tablespoons turmeric
- 2 tablespoons onion powder

Mix all the ingredients together. Stir well. Store in an airtight container for up to 3 months.

CHAPTER 3

Garden Variety

(vegetables)

The coming of age for Gen Xers and Boomers were times of disassociation from fresh whole foods. A social directive for better living through science meant that packaged, frozen, and canned food joined the trends toward "innovation" that affected everything from transportation to community planning to even space travel. The age of Food Industrialization meant that young people became increasingly disassociated from fresh food and where it came from.

Today the story is rapidly changing as young people are taking hold of the helm and steering the ship back to a safe harbor of real, fresh food hallmarked by a largely vegetable diet. In part this is due to attention paid to the childhood obesity epidemic and the impact of food deserts—areas without access to a variety of fresh food markets. As school curricula, nonprofit organizations, White

House directives, and even children's media programs have changed to incorporate learning about healthy food choices and where food comes from, the youngest Americans are being raised with a knowledge of—and appreciation for—fresh food, particularly produce, that is deeper than any recent generation that has come before.

The recipes in this chapter demonstrate a wide range of vegetable offerings, including those not traditionally considered "kid food." You'll find multiple Brussels sprouts recipes as well as those for various squash, okra, and even chile peppers. Simplicity is the hallmark of most of these preparations, most specifically, according to the chefs, to allow the natural flavor of the various vegetables to come through loud and clear.

KEY: **GF** Gluten Free   **VG** Vegan   **V** Vegetarian

Sydney Michael Brown
Fuquay-Varina, North Carolina

In the spring of 2012, Deacon Loretta Hicks of Faith Missionary Baptist Church in Fuquay-Varina, North Carolina, heard about a cooking contest that asked children from around the country to submit a healthy lunch recipe. She approached parishioner Sydney Brown and her family about entering because she knew that the 10-year-old loved to cook. Six months later, the youngster was on her way to the White House as the North Carolina winner of Michelle Obama's Healthy Lunchtime Challenge created in concert with epicurious.com. Her Homerun Meat Loaf Burger (page 162) and Zucchini Fries not only got her invited to the Kids' "State Dinner" held for all winners, but they were also on the evening's menu among the featured dishes. "There's even a picture on the White House website of President Obama trying my zucchini fries!" says Sydney, who is now 12.

The zucchini fries recipe is a lighter version of the homemade French fries usually made by her grandmother, one of the women Sydney says is among her strongest influences in the kitchen, the others being her mother and her great- and great-great-grandmothers. "I have been blessed to have had the privilege to know and spend time with my great-great-grandmother. The first thing she taught me how to cook was a boiled egg and also how to cook collard greens," says Sydney. "Watching my great-great-grandmother in the kitchen at the age of 98 inspired me and gave me the foundation and the tools I needed to learn how to cook."

An excellent substitute for French fries, Sydney's **Zucchini Fries** are best made with smaller zucchini because they contain less water. If you like extra-crispy fries, you can increase the amount of Parmesan cheese to ¾ cup and reduce the breadcrumbs to ¼ cup. For best results make sure to not crowd the fries on the baking pan. Serve with Homerun Meat Loaf Burger (page 162) or Black Bean Salmon Burger (page 131).

ZUCCHINI FRIES

Cooking spray

1 egg white

⅓ cup milk

½ cup grated Parmesan cheese

½ cup plain dried breadcrumbs

¼ teaspoon salt

¼ teaspoon freshly ground black pepper

5 small green or yellow zucchini, peeled and cut into 2 × ¼-inch sticks

1. Preheat the oven to 400°F. Line a baking sheet with parchment paper or coat with cooking spray.

2. In a bowl, combine the egg white and milk. In a second bowl, combine the Parmesan, breadcrumbs, salt, and pepper.

3. Dip the zucchini slices first in the milk mixture and then in the cheese mixture. Shake off any excess and then place the breaded zucchini on the baking sheet in a single layer, without crowding.

4. Bake the fries until they are lightly browned and crispy, 30 to 35 minutes. Serve hot.

Megan Yee
San Francisco, California

Cookbooks were an entrée to reading for 12-year-old Megan Yee who, because of dyslexia, found traditional books more difficult to manage. An exuberant cook who enjoys trying new things, Megan gets inspiration from online cooking sites and from the world around her.

Her culinary style is more "on the fly" when she gets in the kitchen alongside her cooking partner, twin sister Hannah (page 184), for the monthly dinner challenges put to them by their mother since they were in fourth grade.

"I like to make things that sound good. Sometimes they aren't so good but I try anyway," says Megan. Her lunchmeat "sushi rolls" are one example of a dish that wasn't such a hit with her family but, undaunted, Megan, still seeks out the unusual.

"I like trying new things and I will always try a food once. I will try things that my friends and even some of my family will not try," she says.

Her **Napa Cabbage Sauté** is more along the lines of the traditional vegetable stir-fries she learned from her great-grandmother who remained an avid cook for most of her 95 years. Megan's stir-fry is a foundational dish with which more exotic preparations can be made because of the straightforward flavor of mild napa cabbage. Because the olive oil is not just a cooking agent but the carrier of the pungent taste of the garlic and sweetness of scallion, use the best quality olive oil you can find.

NAPA CABBAGE SAUTÉ
SERVES 4 TO 6

1 small head napa cabbage, end trimmed
3 tablespoons olive oil
6 cloves garlic, quartered
3 scallions, green parts only, minced
Salt and freshly ground black pepper

1. Lay the cabbage on its side. Starting at the top of the head (the end opposite the root end), cut crosswise into 2-inch-wide slices until you have sliced three-quarters of the cabbage. You should have mostly green slices of cabbage.

2. Wash the cabbage slices and dry in a salad spinner. The leaves must be really dry.

3. In a large skillet, heat the olive oil over medium heat. Add the garlic and cook for 1 minute, being careful not to let it burn. Add the minced scallions and stir well. Cook 1 minute more or until the scallions have softened.

4. Add the cabbage and lightly stir-fry for 2 or 3 minutes—do not allow the cabbage to wilt. Season with salt and pepper to taste. Serve as a side dish.

John Breitfelder
New Canaan, Connecticut

Ten-year-old John Breitfelder got his start in the kitchen making "Spice Soup" when he was 4. "It was nothing more than my throwing a bunch of spices in a pot with water and walking around the house and asking people to try it," says the chef and Connecticut winner of the First Lady's Healthy Lunchtime Challenge with Epicurious.com.

Six years after making Spice Soup, he's graduated to exploring the farmers' markets in the company of his grandfather, looking for new and unexpected ingredients to experiment with. One farmers' market find—kale—was paired with quinoa to create a "risotto" along with shrimp.

John prepared his creation on some local news programs and later the dish made it into the public schools in his hometown of New Canaan. "Three elementary schools, our middle school, and our high school served it too," he says. "I think it is pretty cool that so many kids ate quinoa and kale for lunch that day! Some kids had never tried either one of them before. It's fun to share new foods with people."

John's pesto recipe deviates from the traditional version because kale and spinach share equal billing with the basil. And because there are no pine nuts, the pesto is lower in fat than usual—all of which leads him to refer to the concoction as a health "superhero."

While vegetarian, John's **Eggplant Pesto Sandwich** is hearty enough for any meat-eater, thanks to thick slices of grilled eggplant and mozzarella cheese. Leah Newton's Mediterranean Bread (page 182) is a good rustic bread to use with this recipe.

(continued)

EGGPLANT PESTO
SANDWICH

1 small Italian eggplant, cut crosswise into 8 rounds (½ inch thick)

1 tablespoon extra virgin olive oil
Salt

¼ cup Superhero Pesto (recipe follows)

8 slices (½ inch thick) rustic whole-grain bread, toasted

4 slices (¼ inch thick) tomato

4 slices (¼ inch thick) fresh mozzarella cheese

1. Preheat a grill to high.

2. Brush the eggplant slices with the olive oil and sprinkle each lightly with salt. Grill the eggplant slices until tender, about 4 minutes on each side. (Alternatively, preheat the broiler and place the eggplant slices on a greased baking sheet or baking dish. Broil until browned and tender, 8 to 10 minutes, turning once halfway through.) Remove the eggplant slices from the heat.

3. Spread the pesto evenly onto all the toast slices. On each of 4 slices of toast, layer 1 slice of tomato, 2 slices of eggplant, and 1 slice of mozzarella. Top with the remaining slices of toast. Slice each sandwich in half and serve.

Superhero Pesto

This recipe will make more pesto than needed for the eggplant sandwiches, but it may be stored in an airtight container in the refrigerator for up to 1 week. Superhero pesto is delicious on both hot and cold pasta as well as other grilled vegetables and meats.

⅔ cup packed deribbed and chopped kale leaves

⅔ cup packed spinach leaves

⅔ cup packed fresh basil leaves

2 cloves garlic, peeled

¼ cup grated Parmigiano-Reggiano cheese

¼ cup extra virgin olive oil

½ teaspoon salt

¼ teaspoon freshly ground black pepper

Place all the ingredients in a food processor. Pulse continuously, pausing to scrape down the bowl with a rubber spatula as needed, until a smooth paste is formed.

Alessandra Ciuffo
Whitestone, New York

With panache and sass enough for someone twice her age, 13-year old Alessandra Ciuffo is a natural in front of the camera. A competitor on multiple cooking shows, including Food Network's *Rachael vs. Guy*, and a demo chef at the NYC Wine and Food Festival with Guy Fieri, Alessandra has also cooked with Food Network celebrity chef Rachael Ray on her talk show. The young teen whose other passion is competitive dance, says that her Sardinian father is her biggest influence in the kitchen.

"He has taught me to be positive, curious, fearless, self-assured, and enthusiastic. He shows me every day that 'life is good,'" she says of her father, Giovanni, who worked in restaurants in Paris, London, and New York while he was a medical student. "As far as food and cooking, he has shown me how to plan, organize, and check for taste. He has also taught me about blending flavors and most of all to be adventurous."

Alessandra credits her dad's unflagging interest in all aspects of food for her own desire to explore the larger food world and her unflappable confidence in the kitchen—as well as on the dance stage.

As part of her explorations, the young cook came up with the idea of recreating broad, flat pappardelle noodles with zucchini, which makes this **Zucchini Pappardelle** ideal for those following gluten-free diets. Her pesto deviates from the traditional versions of her Italian heritage because she uses mint in greater proportions than basil, giving the mixture an incredibly refreshing, light taste. You'll find that the pesto, which can be stored for up to 1 week, is equally delicious on traditional pasta, particularly in cold pasta salads, and as a sandwich condiment.

How to Wash Greens

Greens and green herbs are delicious and versatile, but no one wants to eat the fine grains of dirt that can be hidden between the leaves. Here's a method for washing greens squeaky clean: Fill a large bowl with cold water and separate the leaves of your greens. Place the greens in the cold water and swirl around. Lift the greens out of the water and place in another bowl. It's important that you lift out the greens rather than simply pouring out the water. Dump out the rinsing water and rinse any sediment out of the bowl. Repeat until no more sediment is visible in the water. Dry the greens in a salad spinner.

If washing herbs such as mint, parsley, or cilantro, leave them loosely bundled and, holding them by the stems, swirl them leaves-down in a large bowl of cold water. As with greens, remove the herbs and pour out the water. Dump out the rinsing water and rinse out any sediment. Repeat until no more sediment is visible in the water. Dry the herbs in a salad spinner.

ZUCCHINI PAPPARDELLE

2 large zucchini, ends trimmed

¼ cup extra virgin olive oil

1 teaspoon coarse salt

4 to 5 tablespoons Mint-Basil Pesto (recipe follows)

¼ cup freshly grated Parmesan cheese (or to taste)

1. Hold a zucchini vertically with one end firmly flat against the work surface. Using a wide vegetable peeler, make thin slices of the zucchini from the stem end to the base, working your way around the zucchini and stopping when you reach the seed bed. Repeat for the second zucchini.

2. Place the zucchini "pappardelle" in a medium bowl and add the olive oil and salt. Mix well so that all the zucchini strips are coated.

3. Heat a medium skillet over medium heat and add the zucchini strips. Gently fry the zucchini, stirring carefully so you do not break the strips, until the zucchini begins to soften but does not get brown, about 5 minutes. The zucchini should remain *al dente*.

4. Remove the zucchini pappardelle from the pan and place them on a platter. Add the mint-basil pesto and toss well so that all the pappardelle are evenly coated. Sprinkle with the Parmesan and serve as a side dish.

Mint-Basil Pesto

½ cup pine nuts

1 cup lightly packed fresh basil leaves

2 cups lightly packed fresh mint leaves

2 garlic cloves, chopped

½ teaspoon coarse salt

Squeeze of fresh lemon juice

½ cup extra virgin olive oil

½ cup grated Parmesan cheese

1. In a medium skillet, toast the pine nuts over medium-low heat, swirling or stirring the nuts frequently, until they are golden brown, 3 to 4 minutes. Remove the nuts from the pan and pour them into a food processor.

2. Add the basil, mint, garlic, salt, and lemon juice to the food processor and pulse to chop the ingredients, scraping down the bowl as necessary. With the food processor running, drizzle in the olive oil in a slow, steady stream. Continue pulsing until the mixture is smooth and even.

3. Scrape down the bowl with a rubber spatula, add the cheese, and pulse again to combine fully. The pesto can be stored in an airtight container, refrigerated, for up to 1 week.

Rebecca Ritchie
Blaine, Washington

Thirteen-year-old Rebecca Ritchie is the youngest of three sisters who cook together. The trio dreams of one day having their own food truck to showcase the eclectic mix of dishes they prepare that marries their family's West Indian heritage with their American upbringing. Rebecca most enjoys helping her mom cook for families in need in their community. Collectively, the sisters began to volunteer as cooks for a local shelter in the fall of 2013. "Hearing my mom talk about how many kids don't live in circumstances where good healthy meals are an option has really made me more aware of how lucky I am to have good meals and to have people who care enough to teach me to cook," she says. An avowed tomato-lover, Rebecca's **Tomato Chokha** is common to her mother's native Trinidad, where it is most often served as a vegan main dish. But, she says, research has taught her that there is some version of this dish in numerous cultures where it may also be served as a side dish or a dip. It is also an excellent topping for grilled meats or fish.

Tomato chokha balances the fruity tang of tomatoes and the sweetness of caramelized garlic, with a well-rounded kick from chile pepper. If you aren't a fan of high heat you may want to reduce the amount of scotch bonnet chile pepper by half or even a quarter. Another good substitute is $\frac{1}{2}$ teaspoon chipotle chile powder, which adds further depth to the slight smokiness from the roasted tomatoes. If tomatoes are not in season, this dish is best prepared with canned or jarred fire-roasted tomatoes.

TOMATO CHOKHA

Cooking spray

2 pounds vine-ripened tomatoes, cored

1 small Scotch bonnet chile or other chile of your choice, stemmed

5 cloves Roasted Garlic (page 166)

½ cup finely slivered onions

2 teaspoons ground cumin

2 tablespoons olive oil

Salt and freshly ground black pepper

Naan, roti, pita bread, or pita chips (page 39), for serving

1. Preheat the broiler. Lightly coat a roasting pan with cooking spray.

2. Arrange the tomatoes and chile on the roasting pan and lightly coat the tomatoes with cooking spray as well. Roast the tomatoes and chile right under the broiler until they are charred all around, 7 to 8 minutes.

3. Transfer the tomatoes and chile to a food processor or blender. Add the roasted garlic and blend to a smooth paste, about 1 minute. Stir in half of the slivered onions and set aside.

4. Heat a large skillet over medium-low heat and add the cumin. Cook, stirring with a wooden spoon, until the cumin becomes fragrant, 30 seconds to 1 minute. Add the olive oil to the cumin along with the remaining onion and cook until the onions begin to soften, 1 to 2 minutes.

5. Pour the tomato mixture into the skillet with the onion mixture and stir well. Cook for 3 or 4 minutes. Season with salt and black pepper to taste. Serve hot with naan, roti, pita bread, or pita chips.

Birke Baehr (& Granddaddy)
Black Mountain, North Carolina

Eight-year-old Birke Baehr learned in third grade science class that mercury can kill you. So when he came upon an article discussing mercury in high fructose corn syrup, he was confused. "I asked my mom what high fructose corn syrup was and she said as far as she knew it was something that was used to sweeten soda," says Birke, who is now 15. "My immediate thought was, 'Why is there something that can hurt us in our food?' After that, I started researching how companies grow and process our food and how it eventually ends up on our dinner table." Following his natural curiosity, Birke began a journey to not only explore the American industrial food system but to crusade against its ills, particularly focusing on issues such as genetically modified ingredients and seasonal sourcing.

When he was 11, Birke gave a TEDx Next Generation Asheville talk called "What's Wrong with Our Food System and How We Can Make a Difference." To date, the presentation has had over three million online views. He continues to deliver his local, organic, small-farm-first message through social media and with talks around the country to both farming and nonfarming communities.

The teen believes in *doing* as much as *talking*, and recently he tried raising broiler chickens. "I think that the whole process of raising the birds, harvesting them, butchering and then cooking them made a huge impression on me. I definitely am even more inspired now to know where my food comes from, how it is raised, and finally how it's prepared," he says. "There are so many points along the way where something careless can happen. It made me realize, even more, that people really deserve to eat good food that has been grown or raised in this kind of thoughtful way."

Birke also keeps an organic vegetable garden with the help of his grandfather, and this recipe for fried okra and green tomatoes is a favorite when the garden yields a "mess" of okra. Fried green tomatoes and fried okra are particularly traditional Southern heritage dishes that are most often fried separately as a snack or side dish. Those not accustomed to okra often find the vegetable "slimy," but the key to ensuring that it is not is to cook it in hot oil over high heat. This will also prevent the vegetables from absorbing too much oil.

When Birke makes his **Southern Fried Okra & Green Tomatoes**, he emphasizes using organic ingredients, just as he would do at home, not just for taste but for safety as well. This is particularly true for the cornmeal, since, Birke says, corn is a highly modified crop unless it is heirloom and organic. For the eggs, he says, "I like mine pasture-raised, fed nonGMO feed from a farmer I know."

While fried okra and green tomatoes are most often eaten plain and hot, they may be served with remoulade, spicy mayo, or even Tomato Chokha (page 79) as a condiment.

SOUTHERN FRIED OKRA
& GREEN TOMATOES

SERVES 4 TO 6

½ pound fresh okra, stem ends removed, cut crosswise into ½-inch rounds

1 large green tomato, cut into ½-inch chunks

1 medium onion, chopped

2 large eggs

Salt and freshly ground black pepper

½ cup organic heirloom cornmeal

2 tablespoons all-purpose flour

½ teaspoon aluminum-free baking powder

⅛ teaspoon cayenne pepper

2 to 4 tablespoons organic expeller-pressed coconut oil

1. In a large bowl, combine the okra, green tomato, and onion.

2. In a small bowl, whisk together the eggs and salt and pepper to taste. Pour the eggs over the okra mixture and toss well to coat.

3. In a separate small bowl, mix together the cornmeal, flour, baking powder, and cayenne. Add the cornmeal mixture to the okra mixture and toss to coat evenly with the cornmeal breading. Set aside in the refrigerator.

4. In a large cast iron skillet, heat the coconut oil over medium-high heat until just before it smokes, 2 to 3 minutes. Add a single layer of the okra mixture to skillet and cook until it begins to brown, 2 to 3 minutes. Stir the okra mixture until the okra and tomatoes are nicely browned, about 2 minutes more. Remove the vegetables from the pan and drain on a plate lined with paper towels.

5. Continue to cook remaining okra and tomatoes in single layers until all of the vegetables are cooked. Add additional coconut oil to pan as needed before frying additional layers. Eat hot as a side dish or a snack.

Jonathan Marin
Norwood, New Jersey

As an 11-year-old with Asperger syndrome, Jonathan Marin uses food and cooking as a way to show the feelings that might otherwise be difficult for him to express. "It makes me very happy to cook for my family and see them at the dinner table having a good time," says the young cook who makes these **Baked Beans** to accompany his Marinated Skirt Steak (page 159). "My food shows my family that I love them. My food is my gift to them."

If you decide to use dried beans instead of canned pork and beans to make this recipe, start with 1 cup white or navy beans and soak them overnight (see Using Dried Beans on page 24); add about ¼ cup molasses to the flavoring mix. Jonathan developed this recipe after he realized that he had a personal preference for sweet and spicy flavor combinations—a theme he returns to over and over in his cooking. Simmering the bean mixture over low heat is the key to developing those sweet notes that are the hallmark of classic baked beans. An electric slow cooker is another ideal method for preparing them. If you choose to use a slow cooker, follow the recipe as written thorough step 2, then combine all the ingredients in the cooker and cook on low for 6 to 8 hours. While Jonathan makes these beans to accompany his skirt steak, they are equally good in a classic frank 'n' beans combination or as a side dish at a summer barbecue.

BAKED BEANS

3 slices bacon

½ cup diced ham

½ medium onion, chopped

½ large green bell pepper, chopped

1½ cans (15 ounces each) red kidney beans, rinsed and drained

1½ cans (15 ounce each) pinto beans, rinsed and drained

Half a 15-ounce can pork and beans

¼ cup barbecue sauce

¼ cup ketchup

½ tablespoon yellow mustard

1½ tablespoons brown sugar

1½ tablespoons apple cider vinegar

Salt and freshly ground black pepper

1. Heat a large saucepan or Dutch oven over medium heat. Add the bacon and ham and cook until the bacon is crisp. Remove the bacon and ham from the pot with a slotted spoon, reserving the bacon grease. Chop the bacon into small pieces and set aside with the ham.

2. Add the onion and bell pepper to the pot with the bacon grease and cook until the onion is soft and translucent, about 3 minutes.

3. Add the kidney beans, pinto beans, pork and beans, barbecue sauce, ketchup, mustard, brown sugar, apple cider vinegar, and salt and black pepper to taste. Add the bacon and ham and mix well.

4. Simmer, covered, over low heat for 45 minutes.

Catherine Amoriggi
Warwick, Rhode Island

Seventeen-year-old Catherine Amoriggi is proud of the fact that folks far older than her come to her for cooking tips and lessons. "People come to me for cooking advice. My sister's roommates from college text me asking if they can come over for dinner—of course the answer is always yes," says the Rhode Island native who began blogging about her cooking adventures in 2009. Focused on seasonal and local cooking, Catherine nonetheless has a taste for world cuisine. She likes hot foods because, she says, "Who couldn't do with a little spice in their life?" While she says these **Blistered Hungarian Wax Peppers** are not too piquant for pepper-heads, the uninitiated might find them a tad spicy—a flavor note that is nicely balanced by the fatty saltiness of the feta cheese.

BLISTERED HUNGARIAN WAX PEPPERS WITH FETA

SERVES 4

2 tablespoons extra virgin olive oil, plus more for drizzling

5 Hungarian wax peppers

Sea salt

2 tablespoons crumbled feta cheese

¼ teaspoon grated lemon zest

1. Heat a large cast iron pan over high heat. Once the pan is heated, add the olive oil.

2. Using tongs, carefully add the peppers to the pan. Let them get charred and blistered on all sides, about 4 minutes. This process will happen quickly so keep an eye on the peppers and turn them occasionally, if needed.

3. Using tongs, remove the peppers from the pan and place them on a dish.

4. Season the peppers with sea salt to taste. Drizzle the peppers with a little extra virgin olive oil and top with the feta cheese and lemon zest.

Christopher Chernoff
Powell River, British Columbia, Canada

His combined passion for cooking and dedication to a vegan lifestyle led Christopher Chernoff's Aunt Lisa to entrust him with the preparation of the cake for her wedding. Christopher spent a good part of the last year practicing making the wedding cake, a particular challenge as the 12-year-old vegan strives to make a cake without the dairy or eggs he has been raised not to eat.

"I've learned what happens in factory farms and how animals are treated cruelly there, so I don't use any meat or dairy in my cooking or baking," says the youngster. "That way I'm not supporting the factory farm industry."

An avid cook, Christopher contributes to his household's more quotidian meals as well—when he's not playing hockey, soccer, and volleyball or babysitting.

"Both my parents work, my mom is also going to school, and my brothers and I all play hockey and have after-school activities," he says. "When I get home from school, I have time to get things ready for dinner—that makes it easier for my family." Christopher created his **Butternut Squash & Brussels Sprouts with Toasted Pumpkin Seeds** to make use of two of his favorite vegetables, which counterbalance each other nicely with the sweetness of the butternut squash and the slightly bitter bite of Brussels sprouts. The dill adds a surprisingly refreshing top note to the dish and the roasted pumpkin seeds add a crunchy dimension to the tender vegetables.

Toasting Seeds and Nuts

Pumpkin seeds, slivered almonds, and other nuts are easily toasted right on the stovetop using a dry skillet. Simply heat the skillet over medium-low heat and add the desired amount of seeds or nuts. Stir or swirl constantly so that they do not scorch. Cooking time will vary depending on the seed or nut you are using because of their varying fat content. However, regardless of the seed or nut you are toasting, remove them from the pan immediately when they are golden brown.

BUTTERNUT SQUASH & BRUSSELS SPROUTS WITH TOASTED PUMPKIN SEEDS

SERVES 4

2 cups peeled and cubed butternut squash

3 teaspoons olive oil

Salt and freshly ground black pepper

1½ cups Brussels sprouts, ends trimmed

½ medium onion, diced

1 clove garlic, minced

1 teaspoon chopped fresh dill

2 tablespoons toasted pumpkin seeds

1. Preheat the oven to 400°F.

2. Place the butternut squash pieces in a baking pan or other ovensafe dish in one layer. Add 1 teaspoon of the olive oil and salt and pepper to taste, then lightly mix so that all the pieces are coated. Place the Brussels sprouts in a separate baking dish or other ovensafe dish in one layer. Add another teaspoon of the olive oil and toss well so that all the Brussels sprouts are coated with oil.

3. Bake the squash and Brussels sprouts until just fork-tender, 20 to 30 minutes for the sprouts; 30 to 40 minutes for the squash.

4. While the butternut squash and Brussels sprouts are roasting, heat a medium skillet over medium heat and add the remaining 1 teaspoon oil. Add the onion and garlic and cook, stirring occasionally, until the onions are softened, 2 to 3 minutes. Add half the fresh dill and mix well. Cook for 1 minute more. Remove from the heat.

5. Transfer the roasted squash and Brussels sprouts to a large platter. Add the onion-garlic mixture and mix well. Sprinkle with the remaining fresh dill and roasted pumpkin seeds.

Sarah Rountree
Westport, Connecticut

Sarah Rountree, 17, is a bold-veggie evangelist. The young vegetarian, who lives in Connecticut, says that too often nonmeat dishes aren't treated with the intense flavors and dramatic preparations that would make them most appealing. A volunteer cook for a local homeless shelter as well as the cofounder of a small online bakery, Sarah wants to impart dramatic food experiences to whomever she is cooking for. With an intention of a career in food preparation, the teen takes her inspiration not only from the high school culinary team of which she is a part, but also from chefs she admires both as cooks and as individuals, like Elizabeth Falkner whom she met last year. "The opportunity to get input from someone I admire so much really inspired me to keep working with food," she says. Sarah's signature recipe is roasted, **Crispy Brussels Sprouts** dressed in an addictive warm sauce featuring honey, star anise, and mint. It is based on a dish she had at a New York City restaurant. "These bold flavors really make the Brussels sprouts pop. Even someone who doesn't like Brussels sprouts will like these!" she says.

CRISPY BRUSSELS SPROUTS IN HONEY-MINT SAUCE

SERVES 6

- 3 pounds Brussels sprouts, ends trimmed, quartered
- ⅓ cup olive oil
  Salt and freshly ground black pepper
- ½ cup honey
- 2 whole star anise pods
- ¼ cup fresh lemon juice
- 2 tablespoons chopped fresh mint

1. Preheat the oven to 375°F.

2. Toss the Brussels sprouts in 3 tablespoons of the olive oil and add salt and pepper to taste. Spread the Brussels sprouts in a single layer on a baking sheet or other ovensafe dish and roast until crispy, 20 to 25 minutes, stirring once halfway through.

3. While the Brussels sprouts are roasting, combine the honey and star anise in a small saucepan and heat over low heat for 10 to 15 minutes, swirling the pan as foam forms. Remove from the heat and discard the star anise.

4. In a medium bowl, whisk together the honey, lemon juice, and mint until thoroughly combined, then whisk in the remaining olive oil. Season with salt and pepper to taste.

5. Toss the roasted Brussels sprouts in the honey-mint dressing and serve warm.

Cooking Up Change (the Activists)

Orren Fox

Newburyport, Massachusetts

For some young cooks, preparing food is as much about a social message as it is about the flavors and composition of the dishes themselves. For individuals like anti-GMO activist Birke Baehr (see page 80), nutrition advocate Karthik Rohatgi (recipe page 10), antihunger crusaders McKenna Faulk (page 222) and Catherine Amoriggi (pages 34 and 84), and Leah Newton (page 181) who bakes for the homeless, cuisine is a way to share a point of view that promotes access, justice, and health for all. Add to that list Orren Fox of Massachusetts, who first became interested in the plight of farm animals before he was 10 years old.

"When I was about 9, I went to my babysitter's farm and became really interested in chickens—not to eat, but in them," says 15-year-old Orren, author of the blog *Happy Chickens,* which chronicles his journey into chicken farming and earned him an invitation to the White House for a USDA Know Your Farmer event in 2012. Being around creatures that create food is a passion for Orren, who also started keeping bees when he was 12. "Each egg that a hen lays seems like a real treasure," says the teen, who also contributes blog posts for *Civil Eats* and *HandPicked Nation.* "And bees are critical to one-third of everything we eat with their pollination. The honey is absolute gold. It requires so much work to collect a single teaspoon of honey."

Orren's approach to chicken farming and beekeeping is a purely natural one, eschewing chemical amendments of any kind. "I love going out to the chicken coop or to the beehives to see what all the girls have done. They are hard workers," says the teen who wrote in one blog post that he "believes in the power of women—I work for around a half-million of them every day and they work for me. We take care of each other."

This past year, Orren started keeping bees at his school, harvesting the first batch of honey in the fall. He's been featured on NPR and Greenhorns Radio, and in *Yankee Magazine,* the *Boston Globe,* and others.

While he says he's not much of a cook, focusing instead on harvesting ingredients, he does use the bounty of his hives to enhance the natural qualities of other simple foods such as the sweetness in his **Honey-Toasted Carrots.** The honey helps the carrots caramelize nicely to a toothsome golden brown without being overpoweringly sweet thanks to the salty flavor of soy sauce.

Honey-Toasted Carrots

1 teaspoon salt
1 bunch baby carrots, trimmed
2 tablespoons extra virgin olive oil
2 tablespoons honey
2 tablespoons soy sauce

1. Preheat the oven to 450°F.

2. In a deep saucepan, bring 6 cups water to a boil and add the salt. Add the baby carrots and cook until slightly tender, about 5 minutes.

3. While the carrots are cooking, in a large bowl, whisk together the olive oil, honey, and soy sauce.

4. Drain the carrots, add them to the bowl with the honey mixture, and toss the carrots well so they are completely coated. Arrange the carrots in a single layer on a baking sheet or in an oven-safe baking dish.

5. Roast the carrots until they begin to lightly brown, about 15 minutes.

How to Choose Honey

Teen beekeeper Orren Fox says that not all honey is what it seems. Often the commercially available honey sold in most supermarkets is "ultrapurified," a process that removes much of the pollen deposits that honey aficionados consider desirable. Orren offers these Do's and Don'ts when buying honey:

DO buy honey from a local producer that sells raw honey. This will have the highest local pollen content, which many consider integral to honey's health benefits.

DON'T bother to look for "grades" of honey, the way you would with maple syrup—it's not labeled in that way.

DON'T be surprised if your honey has large crystals—this is common in raw honey.

DO use pasteurized honey for children, seniors, those with immunity issues, or pregnant women.

DO use pasteurized honey for cooked preparations and save the raw for drizzling and maximum taste impact.

DO ask your beekeeper about the nectar sources for his or her bees because this will impact taste. Keep notes on which flower-honeys you like best, for future reference.

Sydney Michael Brown
Fuquay-Varina, North Carolina

"I go to the North Carolina State Fair every year, not just for the rides and the funnel cake, but for the roasted corn," says tween cook Sydney Brown (see her Zucchini Fries, page 71, and Homerun Meat Loaf Burger, page 162). Her cooking style is all about updating down-home favorites for health and flavor. "One day, I thought maybe I could try to make roasted corn in my own unique way." After some experimenting, Sydney came up with what she calls **Fair-Worthy Corn,** which has a similar flavor profile to Mexican seasoned corn, but without the addition of cheese. Instead, a compound or flavored butter is used to elevate the simple sweetness of corn with the spiciness of adobo seasoning, the fresh counterpoint of parsley, and the brightness of lemon pepper.

The complexity of this corn on the cob makes it a stand-alone dish as well as a side dish for traditional barbecue fare. If cooking the corn outdoors on a grill, cook the corn, in their husks, directly on a medium-low grill for 20 minutes. To double or triple this recipe for a larger gathering, simply increase the amount of corn, as you'll only use about one-quarter of the compound butter for four ears of corn. Compound butter is a great flavor enhancer to have on hand and will keep for up to 1 week in the refrigerator. Use it to flavor roast chicken, fish, steamed or roasted vegetables, or mashed potatoes.

FAIR-WORTHY CORN

SERVES 4

- 4 ears of corn, unhusked and rinsed
- 8 tablespoons (1 stick) salted butter, at room temperature
- 1 large clove garlic, finely chopped
- ½ teaspoon seasoning salt
- 1 tablespoon chopped fresh parsley
- 1 teaspoon adobo seasoning, store-bought or homemade (page 65)
- ¼ teaspoon lemon-pepper seasoning

1. Preheat the oven to 350°F.

2. Place the ears of corn in a baking dish or on a baking sheet and place in the oven. Bake for 30 minutes.

3. Meanwhile, in a medium bowl, mix together the butter, garlic, seasoning salt, parsley, adobo, and lemon pepper with a rubber spatula until all the ingredients are evenly blended.

4. Remove the corn from the oven and allow to cool slightly. Peel the husks and silks from the corncobs and arrange on a platter. Spread 1 to 2 teaspoons of the seasoned butter onto the hot corncobs and serve.

Ben Gaiarin
Oakton, Virginia

"I am a chef of the digital age," says Ben Gaiarin, the 16-year-old author of the blog *BenGusto,* which is based on a foundation of the traditional Italian cooking the young man learned from his *nonna* (grandmother) and from frequent summers spent on the Italian Riviera where his extended family, including his grandparents, still live.

As much as Ben feels comfortable in the digital realm, real, personal interactions are his most important influence. Fortunate enough to travel throughout Italy and Europe with his family, which is in the wine industry, Ben says he's been able to learn about truffle hunting, salt farms, grape harvest, olive oil making, and much more—firsthand.

Despite his sophisticated food interactions Ben doesn't take himself too seriously, laughingly recounting his first food experiences being the "chef" at his toy kitchen, serving guests plastic food complete with recommendations for the special of the day. Now, he regularly features "Ben-Gusto Disasters" on his blog. "I laugh, learn from it, and post it on my site so my readers can laugh with me. And when I succeed in making a masterpiece, I jump for joy and share it with the world too," he says.

Ben's **La Peperonata Redux** is a riff on the traditional Italian vegetable dish that is usually made with eggplant as the informing ingredient and is reminiscent of ratatouille. His version, which largely comprises peppers, is lighter and sweeter than the original. This variation, he says, is based on one he enjoyed at a dinner at the home of an elderly Piedmontese neighbor one winter.

The traditional Italian technique of caramelizing the garlic cloves in oil and then removing them infuses the dish with the sweetness of garlic without any of the bitterness that can come from frying the cloves. If tomatoes are not in season, this dish works well with canned or jarred diced tomatoes.

La Peperonata Redux can be served as a side dish or vegetarian main course, along with a loaf of crusty bread.

LA PEPERONATA REDUX

SERVES 6 TO 8

¼ cup extra virgin olive oil

3 cloves garlic, peeled

Dash of red pepper flakes

2 medium yellow onions, sliced into thin rings

2 large yellow bell peppers, chopped

2 large red bell peppers, chopped

1 large orange bell pepper, chopped

2 medium eggplants, finely chopped

2 medium zucchini, finely chopped

14 Roma tomatoes, roughly chopped

3 tablespoons finely chopped fresh basil

1 tablespoon fresh thyme leaves

1 chicken bouillon cube (optional)

Salt

3 tablespoons dried breadcrumbs

1. In a large deep pot, heat the olive oil over medium heat. Add the garlic and pepper flakes, and reduce the heat to low, and cook stirring constantly until the garlic softens, about 2 minutes.

2. Carefully remove the garlic and discard. Add the sliced onions to the hot oil and increase the heat to medium. Stir often until the onions caramelize, 4 to 5 minutes.

3. Add the peppers, eggplants, zucchini, and tomatoes and cook for 2 to 3 minutes. Add ½ cup water and allow to simmer for a few minutes, stirring occasionally.

4. Add the basil and thyme leaves and mix well, then add the chicken bouillon cube (if using). Continue to simmer for another 10 minutes, or until all the vegetables, especially the peppers, have softened and boiled down.

5. When most of the liquid has been absorbed, remove the peperonata from the heat. Add salt to taste and stir in the breadcrumbs.

Mia Alessi
Parkton, Maryland

Mia Alessi is both an entrepreneur and a passionate cook who loves to add modern twists to heritage recipes. The 13-year-old, who has developed her own line of cake mixes under the name "Bratty Crocker," tapped old-school culinary technique to carve an apple-swan when she auditioned for entry to a local magnet high school with a culinary program.

Cooking from the past is particularly appealing to Mia who has adapted her grandfather's 1940s potato cake recipe by adding a little more spice and a crème fraîche dipping sauce to replace everyday sour cream. "My pop pop was a teenager in the 1940s and he worked at a restaurant doing everything from washing dishes to cooking," she says. "He came up with potato cakes as a way to use leftover mashed potatoes." Mia says the secret ingredient to **Pop Pop's Potato Cakes** is something that is often in short supply today: patience. "You have to cook them slow and low to get the perfect golden brown crust and resist the urge to poke at them," she says. "But it's definitely worth the wait."

POP POP'S POTATO CAKES

2 pounds Red Bliss potatoes, scrubbed and diced

2 teaspoons salt

4 tablespoons (½ stick) butter, sliced

½ cup milk

½ teaspoon freshly ground black pepper

½ cup all-purpose flour

½ cup crème fraîche

3 tablespoons chopped fresh chives

½ teaspoon garlic powder

3 tablespoons olive oil

1. In a large saucepan, combine the potatoes, 1 teaspoon of the salt, and enough cold water to cover them by 3 inches. Bring the potatoes to a boil over medium-high heat and boil until tender, 15 to 20 minutes. Drain and return to the pan. Place the saucepan over medium heat and cook for 1 minute so that any excess water boils off.

2. Reduce the heat to low, add the butter, and mash the potatoes until they are smooth. Using a whisk, whisk in the milk until absorbed. Removed the potatoes from the heat and spoon into a heatproof bowl. Allow the potatoes to cool, then refrigerate overnight or for at least 6 hours.

3. In a shallow bowl, whisk together the remaining 1 teaspoon salt, the black pepper, and flour. Set aside.

4. Divide the chilled potato mixture into 8 to 10 even portions. Slightly dampen your hands and form the mashed potatoes into patties, as you would a hamburger. Dredge the potato patties in the flour mixture and shake off any excess flour.

5. Refrigerate for 15 minutes.

6. While the potato cakes are chilling, in a small bowl, mix together the crème fraîche, chives, and garlic powder. Set aside.

7. Heat a large nonstick skillet over medium heat. Add the olive oil, then gently lay the potato cakes in the pan, without crowding them. Cook the potato cakes in two batches, if necessary. Cook the patties until the edges begin to brown, 8 to 10 minutes. Gently flip each patty and cook on the other side until golden and crisp, 8 to 10 minutes.

8. Remove from pan and serve warm with the crème fraîche–chive mixture on the side.

CHAPTER 4

Great Grains

(Pastas/Grains)

Pasta and rice have long been considered the most bland of "kid foods," but the recipes in this chapter demonstrate that nothing could be further from the truth. Showcasing a range of ingredients from whole-grain pasta to risotto and homemade ravioli, these dishes also take a skilled approach to layering flavor, texture, and ingredients to create recipes that are good enough to earn center-of-the-plate status for the most discerning eaters—adult and kid alike. Many of the recipes feature a single-pot cooking style and are ideal for family-style service or for large parties. Gluten-free eaters will find information on gluten-free pastas (page 107) to use for substitutions in these recipes.

KEY: **GF** Gluten Free **VG** Vegan **V** Vegetarian

Taylor Williams
Detroit, Michigan

With a focus on healthy eating, self-agency, and positive economic impact with an underpinning of social good, the nonprofit Detroit Food Academy teaches young people like Taylor Williams how to turn their love of food into a viable future. The 15-year-old enrolled last year in the 25-week afterschool program, which has a final project goal of helping teens launch food-based businesses in local farmers' markets. There, says Taylor, she learned new, healthier twists on the old family favorites she learned in her grandmother's kitchen.

"I learn new things in the kitchen, new recipes, and new ways to grow my experience in food," says the teen, who also says part of her food academy experience was cooking and eating in ways entirely different from her upbringing, like the vegetarian meal she helped prepare at a media dinner. "It opened my eyes to the different ways people eat," she says. The biggest motivation toward her long-term goal of attending culinary school is, she says, "the chance to learn about different foods around the world, not just America but in different countries, and to meet new people."

Taylor knows that positive change comes in both big and small ways and that's why her makeovers of her grandmother's dishes change up just a few items, like substituting whole wheat macaroni for regular macaroni and turkey bacon for pork bacon in her signature **Bacony Mac 'N' Cheese**.

(continued)

BACONY MAC 'N' CHEESE

SERVES 6 TO 8

5 strips turkey bacon

2 teaspoons coarse salt

1 pound whole wheat elbow macaroni

5 tablespoons butter

5 tablespoons all-purpose flour

5 cups 2% milk

4 cups shredded reduced-fat cheddar cheese

Salt and ground white pepper

1. Preheat the oven to 350°F. Line a baking sheet with parchment paper or a silicone baking mat.

2. Place bacon strips on a baking sheet and bake until browned and slightly crispy, about 10 minutes. Remove from the oven (but leave the oven on). When the bacon is cool enough to handle, crumble it into small pieces.

3. In a large saucepan, bring 6 cups water and the coarse salt to a boil. Cook the elbow macaroni according to package directions. Meanwhile, grease a 9 × 12-inch baking dish. Drain the macaroni and transfer to the baking dish.

4. In a medium saucepan, heat the butter over medium-low heat until it is melted. Whisk in the flour and cook, stirring constantly, for 1 to 2 minutes. Do not allow the mixture to brown. Whisking constantly, pour in the milk and cook, whisking, until the mixture begins to thicken, about 1 minute more. Add the cheddar and cook, stirring constantly, until all the cheese is melted. Add salt and white pepper to taste and mix well. Remove from heat.

5. Pour the melted cheese sauce over the macaroni, then sprinkle the bacon pieces on top of the dish. Bake until the macaroni is bubbling and the cheese begins to brown slightly, about 30 minutes.

Hanna Lemaire
Sonoma, California

A Northern California native, Hanna Lemaire says she began cooking at age 5 but really got into the kitchen to be a help and comfort to her mother after her father passed away. "When it became only my mom cooking she needed assistance in the kitchen and I was happy to help," says the 16-year-old whose deep love of her region, with its year-around abundance of fresh produce, has influenced her cooking style. "I am also a sucker for spices and fragrant foods. I love popular dishes with a pop," says Hanna. Being from the California wine country also influences her use of wine in dishes to round out the flavors, as in her vegetable risotto, a dish she says she developed as a sophisticated homage to the "addiction" to plain rice she's had since she was a little girl.

Those familiar with classic risotto preparations that require diligent stirring of the rice grains while adding hot stock or broth in stages, will appreciate the less labor-intensive oven-baked method of Hanna's **Spring/Summer Vegetable Risotto.** However, Hanna stresses the importance of step 5 in the process—adding the remaining stock, wine, salt, pepper, cheese, and butter and stirring briskly for two solid minutes—or the mixture will become gummy instead of creamy.

(continued)

SPRING/SUMMER VEGETABLE RISOTTO

SERVES 8 TO 10

3 tablespoons extra virgin olive oil

1 small white onion, finely chopped

1½ cups Arborio rice

5 cups chicken stock

1 small zucchini, finely diced

1 small butternut squash, peeled and finely diced

½ cup small purple cauliflower florets

1 small yellow carrot, finely diced

1 small orange carrot, finely diced

¾ cup white wine

2 teaspoons salt

½ teaspoon freshly ground black pepper

¾ cup freshly grated Parmesan cheese

4 tablespoons (½ stick) butter, cut up

½ cup peas, fresh (see Note) or thawed frozen

1. Preheat the oven to 350°F.

2. Heat a large Dutch oven or ovenproof saucepan over medium heat. Add 1 tablespoon of the olive oil. Add the onion and sauté until softened and lightly browned, 3 to 4 minutes.

3. Add the rice and stir well so that all the grains are coated with the oil, then pour in 4 cups of the chicken stock. Stir well, making sure that no rice grains stick to the bottom of the pan. Cover and place the pot in the oven. Bake until the rice has absorbed all the cooking liquid, about 45 minutes.

4. Meanwhile, in a large skillet, heat the remaining 2 tablespoons olive oil over medium heat. Add the zucchini, butternut squash, cauliflower, and carrots. Sauté the vegetables until they are browned and slightly softened, about 5 minutes. Remove from the heat and set aside.

5. Take the rice out of the oven and add the white wine, salt, pepper, Parmesan, butter, and remaining 1 cup chicken stock. Stir briskly for 2 minutes with a wooden spoon until combined.

6. Gently stir in the peas and the sautéed vegetables. Season with additional salt and pepper to taste and serve hot.

NOTE: *If using fresh peas, simmer in 1 cup water until just tender, about 10 minutes and drain.*

Remmi Anne Smith
Tulsa, Oklahoma

Remmi Anne Smith is the Student Ambassador for Health and Wellness for the North America division of food service giant Sodexo. Working with the company's executive chefs in 500 schools, Remmi offers a kid's perspective on child nutrition, representing the voice and tastes of three million students. A cook herself, Remmi provides healthy recipes for Sodexo to serve in its 4,000 cafeterias across the country and stars in a twelve-episode cooking series of her own creation that is also aired in the schools.

It all started when the 14-year-old learned about how low her home state of Oklahoma ranked on healthy-state statistics. "So, I decided to do a web series showing other kids how you can cook nutritious foods," she says. "It was my creative way of addressing the childhood obesity epidemic." The series, entitled *Cook Time with Remmi*, has not only earned the teen a place advising Sodexo but has led to numerous local and national television appearances as well.

One of seven children, she is also a representative for the national No Kid Hungry campaign. In addition to learning advanced cooking skills alongside the many chefs that Remmi says have inspired her, she's learned a thing or two about supporting the dreams of others. "I didn't want to wait until I was a grown-up to work towards my dream and there have been so many chefs who have helped make this happen for me," she says. "I want to be just like them when I grow up and I want to support the dreams of young people who have goals just like mine."

Remmi's **Angel Hair Pasta & Tomato/Pancetta Sauce** represents a combination of what she says is her—and a lot of kids'—favorite ingredients: pasta and sauce, but lightened up with fresh tomatoes and made more healthful with the addition of plenty of fresh herbs and baby spinach.

ANGEL HAIR PASTA & TOMATO/ PANCETTA SAUCE

1 tablespoon olive oil

¼ pound pancetta, diced

5 cloves garlic, minced

1 onion, cut into medium/small dice

4 cups grape tomatoes

2½ cups low-sodium chicken broth

¼ cup chopped fresh parsley

¼ cup chiffonade (see page 116) of fresh basil

Salt and freshly ground black pepper

1 pound angel hair pasta

3 cups baby spinach

¾ cup freshly grated Parmesan cheese

1. In medium skillet, heat oil over medium heat. Add pancetta and cook until it starts to crisp, about 2 minutes. Add the garlic and onion and sauté until the onions are soft and translucent, 1 to 2 minutes. Add the tomatoes and chicken broth and reduce heat to a simmer. Cook until the tomatoes have softened, 5 to 6 minutes. Add the parsley, basil, and salt and pepper to taste.

2. While the sauce is simmering, cook the pasta according to package directions and drain.

3. Place the spinach in a loose mound in the center of a large platter. If made ahead, reheat pasta in hot water for 1 to 2 minutes. Pile the pasta in small mounds on the spinach. Spoon the sauce on the pasta and sprinkle with the grated cheese.

Gluten-Free Pastas

Those leading gluten-free lifestyles can easily substitute the pasta in most of these dishes with alternatives that make use of corn, spelt, quinoa, and bean flours. Alternative and natural foods markets often have the widest variety of gluten-free pasta available, including handmade stuffed pastas, but more mainstream groceries are offering options as well. The Food and Drug Administration (FDA) has guidelines for producers when making gluten-free claims, so look for pastas clearly marked with appropriate labeling and follow the package directions when preparing.

Walden Pemantle
Wynnewood, Pennsylvania

Walden Pemantle's love of cooking began when his Kenyan godfather taught him how to make hot fudge upside down cake. The love of cooking sparked by his godfather led young Walden to take every kids' cooking class available at a local culinary school.

"I even took the mother-daughter tea party class," he laughs. By the time he was 12, having run through all the school's offerings, he petitioned them to allow him to take adult courses—beginning with a 12-week French basics course. "I was 13 and the one rule was that I was *not* to try any of the wines," he laughs.

When he isn't cooking or playing competitive Frisbee, Walden organizes lasagna cooking drives at his school to feed hungry families and pairs students in the school's one-to-one mentor program, which matches volunteers with autistic-spectrum students who could use friends and peer-supporters to help them with the socially and academically intense environment.

Walden's **Baked Sweet Pumpkin Ravioli** is his signature dish and one that he most often uses as an *amuse-bouche*. The dish came about during what he calls a particularly awful family dinner made up of freezer leftovers. Most of it was left untouched except for a tray of baked French fries. Walden says that a couple of old frozen tortellini had made their way onto the tray and had baked along with the fries, which made them come out crisp.

"I tried eating them as finger food and they weren't that bad. In fact, dipped in a bit of balsamic vinegar, they were pretty good," he says. "After that, I began experimenting with different types of homemade ravioli, using balsamic glaze instead of vinegar, and tried injecting the glaze into the air cavities formed in the ravioli while crisping them. Eventually, I arrived at the recipe below."

BAKED SWEET PUMPKIN RAVIOLI

SERVES 4

1 large egg yolk

2 tablespoons water

Plain dried breadcrumbs, for dredging

1 pound pumpkin ravioli, store-bought or homemade (recipe follows)

About ⅔ cup balsamic glaze (available in specialty section of most grocery stores)

1 tablespoon fresh lemon juice

1 tablespoon extra virgin olive oil

8 ounces baby arugula

Freshly grated Parmigiano-Reggiano cheese

1. Preheat the oven to 400°F. Line a baking sheet with parchment paper.

2. In a small bowl, beat together the egg yolk and water. Spread breadcrumbs in a shallow bowl for dredging. Dip each ravioli in the egg mixture and then coat with breadcrumbs. Arrange the breaded raviolis on the baking sheet. Bake until the ravioli are golden and toasted, about 15 minutes.

3. When the ravioli are done, remove from the oven and allow to cool slightly. Using a small paring knife, cut a ¼-inch-long slit in the center of each ravioli.

4. Using a squeeze bottle with a narrow tip, or a small spoon, squeeze about ¼ teaspoon balsamic glaze into each ravioli.

5. In a large bowl, whisk together lemon juice and olive oil. Add the arugula and toss well until all the leaves are coated, then arrange the arugula on a platter.

6. Arrange the baked ravioli on top of the baby arugula and sprinkle generously with the Parmigiano-Reggiano to cover the slits in the ravioli. Serve warm.

Pumpkin Ravioli

Filling

- 1 pound piece of cheese pumpkin, seeded, or 1 can (15 ounces) pumpkin puree
- 1 large egg yolk
- 1 tablespoon dried sage
- ¼ teaspoon freshly grated nutmeg
- ¼ teaspoon sea salt
- Freshly ground white pepper
- 1 to 2 tablespoons fine dried breadcrumbs

Dough

- 2 cups all-purpose flour
- 3 large eggs
- 1 tablespoon milk

1. For the filling: Preheat the oven to 400°F. Place the pumpkin on a baking sheet and bake until tender, 1 to 1½ hours. Remove from the oven and cool completely.

2. When the pumpkin is cool, scrape the flesh off the skin and into a food processor. Alternatively, place the pumpkin puree in a fine-mesh sieve and allow some of the liquid to drain, about 10 minutes. Place the drained puree in a bowl and add the egg yolk, sage, nutmeg, sea salt, and white pepper to taste. Mix well. Add 1 tablespoon of the breadcrumbs, only adding more as needed to form a thick paste that does not slip easily off the spoon. Set aside.

3. For the dough: Mound the flour on a clean work surface or in a large bowl and, using a wooden spoon, make a well in the middle of the flour mound. Crack the eggs into the well in the mound and add the milk. Using a fork, slowly draw the flour into the wet ingredients in the well. When all wet and dry ingredients are combined, form the dough into a ball and knead the ball for up to 8 minutes or until smooth and elastic.

4. Once kneaded, roll the dough into an ⅛-inch-thick sheet using a rolling pin or pasta machine.

5. Cut the dough into triangles or squares with equal sides of about 2 inches. Place 1 teaspoon of the filling in the center of a dough triangle/square and place another dough triangle/square on top. Press the triangles/squares together using the tines of the fork. Repeat until all the dough is used up.

The Comfort
of the Kitchen

Georgia Catanese

Wyckoff, New Jersey

For some young people, cooking is more than a hobby, a passion, or a lifestyle—it is a way to overcome very personal physical adversity. Kids like cancer survivor Jack Witherspoon (page 163); food allergy sufferers Tristan Bruni (page 128), Teddy Devico (page 160), and Jacob Shaik (page 151); and Samantha Pecoraro (page 142), who has a rare esophagus disorder that prevents her from actually tasting and swallowing food, demonstrate how the kitchen can provide comfort and empowerment in physically and emotionally painful times.

Georgia Catanese, born profoundly deaf, went through two major cochlear implant surgeries at 15 months old and again at age 7. Throughout this difficult time, Georgia's mom, Donna, was determined that her little girl live a "normal" life and encouraged her interest in cooking, dancing, and sports.

While Georgia excelled at all three, it was cooking that became her obsession, passion, and later her lifeline from grief when Donna was suddenly diagnosed with stomach cancer. She passed away less than a year later, 6 weeks before Georgia's 10th birthday.

Two months later, Georgia's father suffered a major stroke. Suddenly, her avid cooking hobby became a practical necessity as the youngster put the skills her mother taught her to work as a way of helping out. "After Dad got hurt, I started cooking and preparing food for him, so he would eat healthy. I liked it so much that I started trying recipes from various books and the Food Network," says Georgia. As his health improved, Joe Catanese noticed his daughter's passion for being in the kitchen and he encouraged her by signing her up for kids' cooking classes and pushing her skills at home as well.

"My dad and I do *Chopped* type challenges. He gives me a bunch of ingredients and I have to come up with a dish in a specific time—just like on the TV show," she says. "He's not easy on me either," Georgia laughs. "He'll critique the food and take points away if he doesn't think I've done the best I can do."

Today, the teen attends a dual high school program that divides her time between regular high school and an advanced culinary course. While it makes for a hectic schedule—along with managing her own small catering business and updating her adventures on her Facebook page, Teen Chef G—she wouldn't have it any other way because all of it leads toward her bigger dream. One day, Georgia says, she'll open a restaurant, named after her mother. She's already got a folder with clippings of recipes and drawings of the interior—with everything from table arrangements to place settings.

The dish Georgia is most known for is **Jambalaya,** which she first saw on a cooking show when she was 11, and was intrigued by its complexity. "I wanted to challenge myself to not only try it but make it healthier," she says. Georgia's version features brown rice instead of white and chicken sausage patties instead of andouille pork sausage, which is high in fat. The heat that would normally come from spicy Cajun sausage is added with a mixture of cayenne pepper and jalapeños. She first made it for a year-end party for her basketball team when she was just 11.

"My dad was worried no one would like it because of the changes I made," says Georgia. "But the pot was gone before the end of the night."

Jambalaya

- 2 pounds medium shrimp, peeled and deveined, shells reserved
- 1 tablespoon extra virgin olive oil
- 1 pound mild Italian chicken sausage patties
- 2 cups chopped celery
- 2 cups chopped green bell peppers
- 1 cup chopped, red, yellow, and/or orange bell peppers
- 2 cups chopped yellow or white onions
- 2 to 3 teaspoons cayenne pepper (or to taste)
- 3 cloves garlic, minced
- 1 to 2 jalapeño peppers (to taste), seeded and minced
- 1 can (18 ounces) diced tomatoes with garlic
- 2 teaspoons tomato paste
- 2½ cups long-grain brown rice
- 2 cups fat-free low-sodium chicken stock
- 1 teaspoon fresh thyme leaves
- 6 scallions, chopped
- Coarse salt

1. To make shrimp stock, combine the shrimp shells in a large, deep pot with 4 cups water. Bring the water to a boil, turn off the heat, and let sit for 20 to 30 minutes. Reserving the stock, strain out and discard the shells.

2. In large wide pot, heat the olive oil over medium-high heat. Add the chicken sausage and, using a wooden spoon, break meat into small, bite-size pieces and cook until the sausage starts to brown, 8 to 10 minutes.

3. Add the celery, bell peppers, and onions to the pot. Add the cayenne, stir again, and cook until the onions have softened and the mixture is aromatic, about 10 minutes. Add the garlic and jalapeños and cook for 3 to 5 more minutes. Mix in the diced tomatoes and tomato paste. Add the brown rice and stir well, mixing all ingredients.

4. Pour in the 4 cups shrimp stock along with the chicken stock. Add the thyme and scallions. Season lightly with salt and adjust for taste. Cover and cook over medium heat for 40 to 50 minutes.

5. Stir in the shrimp and cook until the shrimp turn pink, about 8 minutes. Remove from heat and let sit covered for 5 to 10 minutes for rice to absorb more flavor and seasoning, then serve.

Anup Ramsundar
Waterloo, Carapichaima, Trinidad & Tobago

When he is not perfecting his technique on the *tabla* (Indian drums) or competing in the ancient art of Sanskrit storytelling, 15-year-old Anup Ramsundar expresses his Hindu faith in the dishes he loves to cook. A camp coordinator for the Chef Leadership camp held by the Growing Leaders foundation, a nonprofit that empowers teens to build self-esteem, Anup experiments with melding modern cooking techniques with the rich vegetarian offerings of his native Trinidad, a country where fully half the population is of Indian descent.

His country also represents a rich mix of cultures and religions. "Even though I'm a Hindu, I am a member of my school's Inter-School Christian Fellowship because I make it a point to not limit myself to one religion but have an open mind towards everything," says the teen who also teaches *tabla* when he's not in the kitchen experimenting with new vegetable dishes.

That open-mindedness has carried over into Anup's culinary style too, as in his **Veggie-Stuffed Pasta Shells** that reinvent an Italian classic using an Indian cheese (paneer) and Caribbean seasonings like culantro. A long-leafed herb that is closely related to cilantro, culantro has less "bite" than cilantro and also doesn't have the "soapy" flavor that some people discern in cilantro.

VEGGIE-STUFFED PASTA SHELLS

SERVES 4 TO 6

2 teaspoons salt

1 box (16 ounces) jumbo pasta shells
Cooking spray

1 teaspoon olive oil

1 small onion, finely minced

2 cloves garlic, finely minced

1 carrot, grated

1 cup frozen seasoned veggie crumbles

1 tablespoon finely minced fresh culantro

1 teaspoon red pepper flakes (or to taste)

¼ cup finely minced green olives (such as Cerignola) or ¼ cup green olive tapenade

¼ cup seasoned dried breadcrumbs

½ cup shredded paneer or Halloumi cheese

½ cup grated Parmesan cheese

1. In a large stockpot, bring 4 quarts water to a boil and add 1 teaspoon of the salt. Add the pasta shells and cook for 10 to 12 minutes. Drain and arrange the shells on a baking sheet.

2. Preheat the oven on 350°F. Coat a 9 × 12-inch baking dish with cooking spray.

3. To prepare the stuffing, heat a large skillet over medium-low heat and add the olive oil. Add the onion, garlic, and carrot and cook, stirring occasionally, until the carrots and onions begin to soften, 5 to 6 minutes. Add the veggie crumbles. Cook for 1 to 2 minutes, stirring occasionally and then add ⅓ cup water. Stir in the culantro, pepper flakes, and remaining 1 teaspoon salt. Allow the veggie mixture to simmer until most of the water is absorbed, 6 to 8 minutes. Remove from the heat.

4. Pour the veggie mixture into a medium bowl. Stir in the olives and breadcrumbs and mix very well. Using a tablespoon, carefully stuff each pasta shell with as much stuffing as it can comfortably hold. Repeat until all the shells are filled, then place the pasta shells in the baking dish.

5. Sprinkle the pasta shells with the paneer and Parmesan. Bake until the cheese is melted and bubbling, 10 to 12 minutes. Serve hot.

Arieanna McKnight
New Orleans, Louisiana

New Orleans teen Arieanna McKnight teaches cooking classes at Kids Rethink New Orleans Schools—or "The Rethinkers," a program created in 2006 to help low-income kids be part of the discussion about how to rebuild the city schools in the aftermath of Hurricane Katrina. The program focuses on everything from school safety to building architecture to school food reform, and has been able to overhaul school lunch programs to be healthier and fresher in the school using a school lunch report card, which assesses the quality of school food.

"I started out as a middle-schooler at the program and now I'm teaching other kids," says Arieanna who is now 17. She says that learning about and becoming an advocate for food justice is one of the most important aspects of her education with the program. Last year the teen cooked with Taste of the NFL in New Orleans, a nonprofit that creates "parties" around National Football League events, with proceeds going to fight hunger in the community.

But, Arieanna says, her greatest influence is her father who works as a chef in New Orleans's French Quarter. "I live in a low-income family and we don't always have as many things to work with," says the teen. "I've watched my father always make us something good to eat, even if he didn't have regular ingredients. It's taught me to be creative with what I have." Arieanna's **Shrimp Pasta with Classic Vinaigrette** is her unique take on a classic New Orleans shrimp pasta salad. She uses crab boil to give the shrimp an intense flavor. Since local and seasonal eating is an important part of how she has come to rethink food, Arieanna uses Gulf shrimp for this recipe.

Making a Chiffonade

To make a "chiffonade," you stack the leaves of fleshy herbs (like basil) or other greens on top of one another and then tightly roll them up into a little cylinder. Using a sharp knife, cut the cylinder crosswise into narrow slices. When the slices are unfurled, you'll have thin slivers of herb or green. That is the chiffonade.

SHRIMP PASTA WITH CLASSIC VINAIGRETTE

Vinaigrette

2 cloves garlic, minced

2 teaspoons minced shallots

2 teaspoons minced fresh parsley

1 teaspoon grated lemon zest

2 tablespoons coarse-grain mustard

Juice of 1 lemon

½ cup white balsamic vinegar

1 cup extra virgin olive oil

Salt and freshly ground black pepper

Pasta

1 teaspoon salt

1 tablespoon extra virgin olive oil

1 pound pasta of your choice

Shrimp

1 pound large Gulf shrimp, peeled and deveined

1 tablespoon crab boil seasoning (such as Old Bay)

1 large tomato, diced

6 fresh basil leaves, cut into a chiffonade, for garnish (optional)

1. For the vinaigrette: In a small bowl, whisk all the ingredients together and set aside.

2. For the pasta: In a large pot, bring 4 cups of water to a boil over medium heat. Add the salt and olive oil. Add the pasta and cook to al dente according to package directions (the time will vary according the type of pasta you choose). Drain and transfer to a large deep platter or pasta bowl.

3. Meanwhile, cook the shrimp: Place the shrimp in a medium saucepan with just enough water to cover them. Stir in the crab boil seasoning and bring the mixture to a boil. Cook until the shrimp turn just pink, 3 to 4 minutes. Drain the shrimp and add to the pasta.

4. Add the vinaigrette to the pasta and shrimp and toss well. Add the diced tomato, toss again, and garnish with basil leaves, if desired.

Eliana de Las Casas
Harvey, Louisiana

Eliana de Las Casas, or Kid Chef Eliana, as she is best known, boasts a schedule as rigorous as any adult celebrity chef. Eliana, who is 14, began blogging and filming YouTube cooking tutorials for people her own age when she was 8 years old. She has also written three cookbooks published by a local New Orleans publisher, all under the "Cool Kids Cook" moniker. A many-time guest on *The Wendy Williams Show* and host of her own VoiceAmerica Kids radio show, also called *Cool Kids Cook*, Eliana has interviewed notable adult chefs like José Andrés, John Besh, Jacques Torres, and several Food Network and Cooking Channel personalities.

A true child of the American experience, Eliana, who counts Cuban, Honduran, Cajun, and Filipino in her background, says, "I love cooking foods from my family heritage. I know a lot about Latino food, Cajun food, and Asian food." Despite her many public achievements, touching others with her food is the ultimate goal, whether that be her family sitting around the dinner table, a TV or radio audience, or local people in need.

"I am part of Builders Club at school," she says. "Once a month, we get together and make sandwiches for the homeless, preparing 300 sandwiches for 150 lunch bags for the men of Ozanam Inn shelter in New Orleans," she says.

Eliana's **Pastalaya** is her own twist on jambalaya—arguably the most famous dish of her native New Orleans—in which she substitutes linguine for rice. The pasta offers a lighter counterpart to the robust flavors from the pork andouille and Creole seasoning.

PASTALAYA

1 pound linguine

2 tablespoons butter

1 pound boneless, skinless chicken breast, cut into ½-inch cubes

1 pound andouille or smoked sausage, cut into ½-inch rounds

⅔ cup chopped green bell pepper

⅔ cup chopped onion

⅔ cup chopped celery

2 cloves garlic, minced

2 cups diced tomatoes

1 cup chicken broth

2½ tablespoons Creole seasoning blend

2 scallions, chopped

Salt

1. Cook the linguine according to package directions; drain and set aside.

2. Heat a large, deep pot over medium heat and add the butter. When the butter is melted, add the chicken and sausage and cook until lightly browned, 10 to 12 minutes. Remove the browned chicken and sausage from the pot using a slotted spoon and set aside.

3. Add the bell pepper, onion, and celery to the pot and sauté until softened, 3 to 4 minutes. Stir in the garlic, tomatoes, chicken broth, and Creole seasoning. Return the chicken and sausage to the pot and increase the heat to medium-high in order to bring the mixture to a boil. Reduce the heat to medium-low, cover, and simmer until chicken is cooked through, about 15 minutes.

4. Add the cooked linguine and scallions and combine thoroughly. Add additional Creole seasoning, if desired, and salt to taste.

CHAPTER 5

The Meat of the Matter

(Fish/Chicken/Meat)

Variety, diversity, and experimentation are large themes in this cookbook and nowhere is that more evident than in this chapter on meat, fish, and poultry. It's here that the dynamic skill and curiosity of the young chefs are most evident in their dishes, which span a range of proteins from simple chicken to smoked ribs, whole roasts, and even game meats.

The wide variety of seafood (including alligator) is particularly worth noting, signaling as it does what may become a fundamental change in the way we, as Americans, interact with seafood—which is to say not too much.

There is another theme among these dishes as well: a taste for spice and heat that mirrors the changing palate of the nation. This new spicy taste profile is based upon the influence of the growing multi-ethnic community in which more and more of America's young people are being raised.

KEY: **GF** Gluten Free **VG** Vegan **V** Vegetarian

Sophia Hampton
Westport, Connecticut

Although an enthusiastic cook today, Sophia Hampton began cooking at age 5 more out of practicality than passion. "We lived in New Mexico and my dad, a man who likes his meat, usually cooked dinner," says the high school junior. "I really did not like the various beef or other meat stews he would make, which were too hearty for my taste, so I decided to try and make my own dinner." Some of those early recipes included fried eggs on blue corn tortillas, smoked oysters on plain crackers, and, later, homemade pesto using basil from the family's garden. Those meals were always hallmarked with what the teen now realizes was an early taste for pure and simple foods. But that doesn't mean she won't indulge when the dish warrants. "My cooking motto is everything in moderation, including moderation," says Sophia. "For example, if I'm going to make a chocolate cake, then I want buttery buttercream, creamy ganache, and fluffy layers."

Her **Delicata-Crab Hash with Poached Duck Egg** is a recipe born of her comfort with experimentation and her love of luscious foods. Sophia has chosen to moderate the meaty undertones of this dish by using turkey instead of pork bacon; it is also a way of preserving the delicate sweetness of the crab as the main flavor profile. Peppered bacon tastes best with this recipe, because it provides just enough bite to contrast with the creamy, fatty flavor of the duck egg. If you can't find duck eggs, a chicken egg will certainly do, although you may want to drizzle a teaspoon of melted butter over the finished hash to make up for lower fat content of a chicken egg.

DELICATA-CRAB HASH WITH POACHED DUCK EGG

SERVES 2

2 tablespoons butter

1 delicata squash, peeled, halved, and cubed

1 pound shiitake mushrooms, stems discarded, caps cut into ¼-inch slices

3 strips turkey bacon

½ pound cooked crab meat (lump or claw)

2 tablespoons extra virgin olive oil

2 duck eggs or chicken eggs

1 teaspoon butter (optional if using chicken egg), melted

1. In a large skillet, heat butter over medium heat. Add the squash and mushrooms and cook, stirring occasionally, until the squash begins to cook through, about 15 minutes.

2. Meanwhile, in a separate skillet over medium heat, cook the turkey bacon until crispy, 5 to 7 minutes. Remove from the pan and place on a plate lined with paper towels. When the bacon is cooled, crumble it into small pieces.

3. Stir the crab and bacon into the squash mixture and toss together well. Add the olive oil and continue to fry the mixture over medium until everything is lightly browned, about 10 minutes more.

4. Meanwhile, to poach the eggs, crack one egg into each of 2 small, microwaveable bowls, being careful not to crack the yolks. Gently add ⅓ cup water to each bowl and cover with a microwaveable saucer. Microwave the egg bowls in 20-second intervals on 75% power. The eggs should be poached within 1 minute.

5. Divide the delicata hash between 2 soup plates and gently remove each egg from its poaching bowl with a slotted spoon and ladle it gently on top of each bowl of hash, being careful not to break the yolk. (If using a chicken egg, drizzle melted butter on top.)

A Place at the Table (Kid Food Critics)

The Regnante Brothers

Ellicott City, Maryland

Even if they aren't cooks, these young people are making their voices heard in the food world. Tween food critic Wyatt Roe reviews restaurants around his South Florida home on his blog *Wyatt Tastes Good*. While he says he doesn't think a "12-year-old reviewing food will change anyone's life," his blog, chronicling his adventures eating out, has earned him a spot on local television.

Another young food reviewer, Elijah Knauer from Maryland, who is also 12 years old, offers his peers kid-friendly restaurant options on his blog *Adventures of a Koodie*. Elijah, who says he has a very developed palate, might try his hand at culinary camp next year.

Also in Maryland, 16-year-old Charles and 14-year-old Thomas Regnante blog their restaurant adventures on *2 Dudes Who Love Food*, which they began 3 years ago as a creative writing project. "The topic of food was the easiest thing for us to write about because we come from an Italian-American family and food is a central part of our cultural life," says Charles. The blog offers restaurant reviews that the boys feel other teens will be able to relate to. Over time they've gone from simply reviewing others' foods to sharing their own recipes and chronicling the food-based community outreach work they do. "Of all the work we've done on our blog, we're most proud of our food philanthropy programs—it's a way to give back to those in need in our community," they say. "At our first event, we raised 200 dollars selling homemade cookies and water. The money helped a group of homeless men make a deposit on a rental home."

The brothers' other activities include a yearly food drive for the homeless and, in 2013, they used their Christmas money to buy water for local animal shelters when the town water sources were contaminated by a chemical spill. After getting others involved in the water drive through their blog, the pair was able to donate 2,000 gallons of water to shelters throughout the area.

Charles and Thomas have been deeply involved in launching a teen foodie website and app with recipes and restaurant reviews that they've developed. "It will be a place for young people to share, learn, and connect," they say. "Our long-term goal with food is to continue to try as many different foods as we can and to one day pass down our love of food to our own kids."

The Regnante brothers are huge flounder fans and their **Vegetable-Parmesan Crusted Flounder** is an adaptation of a dish created by their grandmother. The topping is excellent for use in stuffed clams as well.

Vegetable-Parmesan Crusted Flounder

SERVES 6 TO 8

Fish

Cooking spray

8 pieces flounder fillet
(about 6 ounces each)

¼ teaspoon garlic salt

Freshly ground black pepper

Toppins

2 tablespoons extra virgin olive oil,
plus more as needed

5 cups chopped onions

2 cups chopped celery

2 cloves garlic, finely chopped

¼ teaspoon garlic salt

Freshly ground black pepper

1½ cups seasoned dried breadcrumbs

¾ pound cherry tomatoes, halved or
quartered

½ cup freshly grated Pecorino
Romano cheese

1. For the fish, preheat the oven to 400°F. Line a baking sheet with foil and coat lightly with cooking spray.

2. Pat the fish dry and season with the garlic salt and black pepper to taste. Arrange the fish on the baking sheet. Do not let the fish overlap. Bake until the fish is partially cooked, 7 to 8 minutes. Do not allow the fish to cook completely; it cooks more after the topping is added.

3. Meanwhile, for the topping: Heat a large skillet over medium heat and add the olive oil. Add the onions, celery, and garlic and increase the heat to medium-high. Add the garlic salt and pepper to taste, and sauté, stirring occasionally, until the vegetables begin to soften, 5 to 7 minutes. Reduce the heat to medium-low and cook, stirring occasionally, until they are browned and caramelized, 5 to 7 minutes more. Watch the vegetables carefully and add a little more olive oil if they look dry.

4. When the vegetables are caramelized, add the breadcrumbs and the chopped tomatoes. Stir the mixture carefully so as not to smash the tomatoes. Cook for 1 to 2 minutes more and remove the pan from the heat. Lightly stir in the Romano.

5. Divide the vegetable-cheese topping evenly among the fish fillets. Bake for another 7 minutes. Turn the oven to broil and broil the fish for 5 minutes in order to lightly crisp the breadcrumb topping.

Tristan Bruni
Oakland, California

Suffering from celiac disease encouraged young Tristan Bruni to explore new ways of cooking to satisfy what he calls his "love of enjoying food." Those explorations led the young boy to begin assisting his mom in the kitchen while he was still a preschooler, and then to his participation in a local Iron Chef Kids competition at 8 years old, making it to the finals. The following year, Tristan won the competition neatly; his recipe included a secret ingredient and a strictly timed 30-minute limit. Now a volunteer sous-chef for several local Catholic charities, 12-year-old Tristan particularly likes cooking the Latino and Asian foods of his Mexican grandfather and Japanese/Filipino grandmother. His **Two-Miso Glazed Salmon** came about when his dad returned from a fishing trip to British Columbia with a plentiful catch and the young cook was experimenting with Asian-style ways of preparing this classic North American fish.

Serve the salmon with Quinoa Salad with Fire-Roasted Pepper Sauce (page 28) or Zucchini Pappardelle (page 77).

TWO-MISO GLAZED SALMON   SERVES 4

- 2 tablespoons gluten-free low-sodium tamari
- 2 tablespoons brown sugar
- 3 tablespoons sake
- 2 tablespoons yellow miso paste
- 1 tablespoon red miso paste
- 1 inch fresh ginger, peeled and finely grated
- 4 skin-on salmon fillets (6 to 8 ounces each), rinsed and patted dry
- 2 tablespoons sesame seeds

1. In a medium bowl, whisk together the tamari, brown sugar, sake, miso pastes, and ginger. Divide the mixture in half.

2. Place the salmon fillets in a shallow dish and pour half the miso mixture over them. Refrigerate and allow to marinate while you prepare the sesame seeds.

3. In a small skillet, toast the sesame seeds over medium-low heat. Swirl the pan around, keeping an eye on the seeds to ensure they do not burn as they toast quickly. Once the seeds are golden brown, remove from the pan and set aside.

4. Preheat the broiler. Line with parchment or lightly grease a broilerproof baking dish that will hold all of the salmon fillets with about ½ inch space between them.

5. Remove the salmon from the refrigerator and place in the baking dish, skin-side down and ½ inch apart. Broil the salmon 5 to 6 inches from the heat for 3 minutes, then brush or spoon some of the reserved miso glaze on top of each salmon fillet and return to the broiler for 3 minutes. Brush with the glaze again and broil the salmon until the glaze is sizzling and the salmon meat can just about flake apart with a fork but is still moist inside, about 5 minutes more. Sprinkle with the toasted sesame seeds.

6. Arrange the cooked salmon fillets on a platter and serve.

Hanalei Edbrooke
Cupertino, California

Hanalei Edbrooke is passionate about two things: snowboarding and cooking healthy meals every night for her family. Both snowboarding and cooking, she says, present challenges that can be overcome by finesse, skill, and focus. "I take recipes from websites or books and try to adapt them to be healthier," says the 16-year-old. "I most often look for rich and calorie-laden recipes, such as tiramisu or stuffed sole or creamy soups, and challenge myself to adapt them to be just as good if not better without just adding butter and sugar."

Hanalei chronicles her cooking experiences on her YouTube channel *The Green Beanie*. Her brother is the cameraman.

In 2013, the competitive snowboarder used her YouTube channel to offer her cooking services for family and friends as a way to earn money to fund the siblings' mission trip with their church. "The cost was about $600 per person, but I managed to raise enough money for both of us to go and help build housing for Navajo families in New Mexico," says Hanalei, who hopes to continue cooking to earn pocket money. But even if that doesn't pan out, she says, "I'll still cook for my family every day."

Hanalei created her **Black Bean Salmon Burger** as a lighter version of traditional hamburger with just as much protein punch—a necessity for any athlete. Between the ingredients and the fact that burgers are baked and not fried, there is little fat in these patties over and above the natural fat in the salmon. These burgers may be served in a small whole wheat pita bread, with grilled vegetables or salad as a side dish. They are particularly good topped with guacamole or salsa and served with Zucchini Fries (page 71).

The Secret in the Can of Salmon

Fresh food purists and fish aficionados may blanch at the idea of using canned salmon in this or any recipe, but American canned salmon has a special secret: Most of the stock comes from the far reaches of Alaska from where shipping fresh or even frozen fish proves too costly. Canning is the most common use for this grade of salmon, which includes the prized Copper River and King salmons that fetch the heftiest prices as fresh fillets in gourmet markets.

BLACK BEAN
SALMON BURGER

MAKES 4 LARGE OR 6 MEDIUM BURGERS

Cooking spray

1 small yellow onion, finely chopped

4 cloves garlic, peeled

½ cup chopped fresh cilantro

1 can (15 ounces) black beans, rinsed and drained

1 can (15 ounces) salmon, liquid drained

1 to 2 teaspoons ground cumin (to taste)

1 can (6 ounces) tomato paste

1 teaspoon coarse salt

Juice of ½ lemon

¼ teaspoon cayenne pepper or 1 small jalapeño pepper, seeded and minced (optional)

Breadcrumbs or oat bran, as needed

1. Preheat the oven to 400°F. Line a baking sheet with parchment paper and coat lightly with cooking spray.

2. In a food processor, combine the onion, garlic, cilantro, and beans and pulse until they are shredded and mixed but not completely pureed, 15 to 20 seconds.

3. Transfer the bean mixture in a medium bowl. Add the salmon and mix well. Add the cumin, tomato paste, salt, lemon juice, and cayenne or jalapeño (if using). Mix until all the ingredients are well combined.

4. Form the salmon mixture into 6 to 8 burgers, depending on how big you want them. If they do not hold together well, add breadcrumbs or oat bran to the mixture, a teaspoon at a time, until the mixture binds and can hold the shape of a burger. You should not have to use more than ¼ cup of breadcrumbs or oat bran in the entire mixture.

5. Arrange the burgers on the baking sheet, leaving ½ inch of space all around them and coat each of the burgers lightly with cooking spray. Bake the salmon burgers for 20 minutes then set the oven to broil and broil for 2 minutes to lightly brown the tops of the burgers.

Christina Sylvestri
Meriden, Connecticut

Christina Sylvestri first learned to cook at the side of her grandfather who was a Latino chef, but it wasn't until she found her way to My City Kitchen in Meriden, Connecticut, when she was 15 years old that the high school junior began to take cooking seriously. "Chef Kashia is very motivating. If you mess up, she tells you like it is, but she's still encouraging in a way that makes me want to keep going," says Christina of My City Kitchen's chef and founder Kashia Cave.

For teens like Christina, the nurturing and safe environment the chef provides is even more valuable than the solid culinary skills they learn in the program.

Christina came to My City Kitchen after being placed in foster care away from her hometown after her mother ceased being able to care for her. "The program has also opened my eyes to new cultures and new styles of food," says Christina who wants to delve more into multinational cooking.

She recently fell in love with curries thanks to a shrimp dish she learned from her foster mother, Mervis Sherwood, who is from Jamaica. Christina counts her **Curried Shrimp** as the cornerstone to her growing list of international specialties. It's important, she says, to find Jamaican or West Indian curry powder, which is not as hot as traditional Indian varieties. This dish depends, instead, on a fresh Scotch bonnet or other chile pepper for heat according to the cook's taste. The dish is finished with a classic French technique: *monté au beurre*, which calls for mixing a small amount of butter into the sauce for shine, thickening, and flavor.

Serve the curry with white or brown rice and a green salad.

(continued)

CURRIED SHRIMP

- 2 pounds medium shrimp, peeled and deveined
- ½ teaspoon salt
- ½ teaspoon freshly ground black pepper
- 1 small Scotch bonnet or other chile pepper, thinly sliced
- 1 small green bell pepper, finely chopped
- 1 tablespoon cornstarch
- ¼ cup sunflower oil or other light vegetable oil
- 2 medium yellow onions, finely chopped
- 3 scallions, finely chopped
- 4 cloves garlic, minced
- 3 tablespoons Jamaican curry powder
- 3 tablespoons lemon juice
- 2 tablespoons butter

1. In a medium bowl, combine the shrimp, salt, black pepper, chile pepper, and bell pepper and mix well. Sprinkle with the cornstarch and toss well. Set aside.

2. Heat a medium skillet over medium-low heat and add the oil. Add the yellow onions and scallions and cook until the onions begin to soften, 2 to 3 minutes. Add the garlic and cook 1 minute more.

3. Stir in the Jamaican curry powder and cook, stirring constantly, until the curry begins to release its aromas, about 30 seconds. Add the shrimp and peppers to the curry mixture and cook, stirring occasionally until the shrimp just turns pink, about 5 minutes. Pour in the lemon juice and stir well.

4. Add the butter and stir gently until the butter is melted.

Myka Smith Jackson
Lexington, Kentucky

For Myka Jackson, the Kentucky winner of the Epicurious.com's Healthy Lunchtime Challenge, the best part of the experience was getting to tour the White House Garden with First Lady Michelle Obama. Myka, who is 10, is also a fan of touring the local farmers' markets in her hometown as well as checking out traditional supermarkets for new produce and other fresh ingredients she may not have tried before. "What I like best is talking to the local farmers and learning how they get fresh produce to the farmers' market," she says. While college is many years away yet, Myka already knows she wants to focus on a combination of business, marketing, and food education—particularly as a way to help families in need become self supporting by growing their own foods. Her **Garlic Shrimp & Grits** is her evolution of a family favorite traditionally prepared by her great uncle. Aficionados of this classic Southern dish will note the absence of tomato or spicy sausage in the preparation, which makes for a repast light enough for any time of year.

GARLIC SHRIMP & GRITS   SERVES 4

Grits

6 cups chicken stock or water

1 cup grits

1 teaspoon salt

½ teaspoon freshly ground black pepper

1 tablespoon unsalted butter

Shrimp

1 pound large shrimp, peeled and deveined

Salt and freshly ground black pepper

2 tablespoons unsalted butter

2 large cloves garlic, minced

⅛ teaspoon cayenne pepper

2 tablespoons chicken stock or water

Juice of ½ lemon

2 tablespoons chopped fresh parsley

1. For the grits: In a medium saucepan, bring the stock or water to a boil and slowly whisk in the grits, stirring constantly. Add the salt and black pepper, reduce the heat to low, and simmer, stirring occasionally with a wooden spoon, until tender and thickened, about 30 minutes. Stir in the butter and season with more salt and pepper to taste. Cover to keep warm and set aside.

2. For the shrimp: Sprinkle shrimp with salt and pepper to taste. Melt the butter in a large skillet over medium heat. Add the garlic and cayenne and mix well. Add the shrimp and cook, stirring once or twice until the shrimp turn pink, 3 to 4 minutes. Add the stock or water, lemon juice, and parsley and mix well.

3. Spoon the grits into a wide bowl or high-sided platter and arrange the shrimp on top.

Kristopher DiGiulio
Kirkland, Washington

Growing up in his grandparents' Kirkland, Washington, home, Kristopher DiGiulio learned to cook on the woodstove that shares kitchen space with both an electric and gas range. After a first foray into cooking on the stove at age 9, the now-13-year-old Kristopher went on to be a competition chili cook-off winner and penned a self-published pamphlet of family recipes that he sells with partial proceeds going to the local Shriners children's hospital. He also has a small catering business, providing luncheons for the local Masonic Lodge.

For Kristopher, cooking is also a way to overcome certain food aversions. "For a long time I did not like tomatoes in a sauce because I'd gag and I couldn't swallow it," he said. "I've learned to peel the skin when I cook with tomatoes to solve that problem because they are the most important ingredients in my signature dishes," he says.

Besides chili, Kristopher counts gumbo as one of those signature dishes and one that he is constantly perfecting in order to compete in gumbo cook-offs. His favorite version uses alligator, a protein that captured his imagination because of its exotic nature to most eaters, particularly in suburban Washington State where he makes his home—something he hopes will impress the judges at his next competition.

The alligator, which largely tastes like chicken, can toughen easily so it's important to not overcook the gumbo. Serve **Alligator Gumbo** garnished with fresh parsley over plain rice or with toasted Mediterranean Bread (page 182).

ALLIGATOR GUMBO

2 tablespoons all-purpose flour

6 slices fatty bacon

1 pound andouille or other spicy pork sausage, cut into ½-inch pieces

1 cup chopped onion

½ cup chopped green bell pepper

½ cup chopped celery

6 cups oyster or clam juice

2 cups stewed, peeled, and diced tomatoes

1 pound alligator tail meat, cut into ½-inch pieces

2 teaspoons salt

½ teaspoon freshly ground black pepper

½ teaspoon cayenne pepper

1 tablespoon filé powder

1½ cups fresh okra, trimmed and cut into ½-inch slices

3 sprigs fresh thyme

3 tablespoons chopped fresh parsley

1. To toast the flour, place in a small skillet over medium heat and cook, stirring often, until it becomes dark golden brown. Remove the skillet from the heat and scrape the flour into a small heatproof bowl. Set aside.

2. In a large, deep pot over medium-high heat, add the bacon and andouille and cook until the bacon is crispy and all the fat is rendered out, 5 to 7 minutes. Remove bacon slices and andouille and reserve the fat. Set aside the andouille for the gumbo. (Save the crispy bacon to use in salads or sandwiches.)

3. Reduce the heat to medium and add the onion, bell pepper, and celery to the pot. Cook until the onion begins to soften, 3 or 4 minutes. Add the toasted flour, mix well, and cook for 1 minute, stirring constantly. Pour the oyster or clam juice into the flour mixture, stirring constantly. Simmer until the liquids just begin to thicken, 2 to 3 minutes. Add the tomatoes and stir well.

4. Return the andouille to the pan along with the alligator meat, salt, black pepper, cayenne pepper, and filé. Mix very well and add the okra and fresh thyme. Reduce the heat and simmer, uncovered, until the liquid mixture is reduced by half into a thick stew, about 1 hour 30 minutes. Sprinkle with parsley and serve.

Alex Biedny
Forest Lake, Minnesota

Two Kids Cooking is the name of 11-year-old Sophia and 15-year-old Alex Biedny's brother-sister team's website, YouTube channel, Facebook page, and Pinterest board. Following the youngsters' adventures exploring the food world in a fun—and sometimes goofy—way, their TV program "shows that kids can cook decent food and that it isn't that hard," says older brother Alex.

Not just about having fun whipping up delicious goodies, the show features a "Mad Kitchen Science" section that teaches culinary science, from the chemical reactions that make bread rise to how acids and milk curdle to make cheese and how emulsions like aioli form. While sister Sophia is more of a baker, Alex is a savory cook who says that he learned his credo of "simple is best" on a family camping trip.

"Even with simple cooking appliances and methods, you can create delicious food," he says. "I've come to consider cooking a talent I will always have and that has made me unafraid of trying new foods or techniques."

Alex's **Secret Recipe Chicken Strips** came about one evening while helping his mother quickly get dinner on the table. The recipe is hallmarked by a simple cooking technique that Alex espouses and features spices and flavorings that most people have in their pantry. The saltine crackers make for an extra crispy coating without the need for deep-frying that most chicken fingers or "strips" undergo. Italian seasoning mix is integral to providing a flavor beyond simple breaded chicken. These strips are equally good hot or cold on top of a salad or tucked into a sandwich with fresh greens.

SECRET RECIPE CHICKEN STRIPS SERVES 4

2 eggs

1 teaspoon minced garlic

⅔ cup all-purpose flour

1 sleeve saltine crackers, crushed into meal

2 tablespoons Italian Seasoning Mix (recipe follows)

½ teaspoon salt

1 teaspoon garlic powder

Freshly ground black pepper

2 pounds boneless, skinless chicken breast, cut into 2-inch-wide strips and lightly pounded

½ cup extra virgin olive oil

1. In a wide shallow bowl, beat the egg and minced garlic together. In a second shallow bowl, mix together the flour, saltines, Italian seasoning, salt, garlic powder, and pepper to taste.

2. Dredge each chicken strip in the egg mixture and then in the saltine mixture, making sure both sides are evenly coated. Place the breaded strip on a wide platter and repeat until all the chicken strips are coated. Refrigerate for 15 minutes.

3. In a large skillet, heat the olive oil over medium-low heat. Test the oil by dropping a pinch of flour into the oil. If it sizzles immediately, the oil is ready. Working in batches if necessary, gently lay the chicken strips in the hot oil, being careful to not crowd them in the pan. Fry the strips until golden brown and crispy, 8 to 10 minutes per side. Remove cooked strips from pan and lay them on a platter lined with paper towels to absorb the oil. Serve hot.

Italian Seasoning Mix

MAKES ABOUT ½ CUP

1 tablespoon dried basil

1 tablespoon dried oregano

½ teaspoon dried rosemary

1 tablespoon dried thyme

2 tablespoons dried parsley

1 tablespoon dried marjoram

1 teaspoon paprika

1 teaspoon garlic powder

2 teaspoons salt

1 teaspoon freshly ground black pepper

Mix all the ingredients together and store in an airtight container for up to 2 months.

Samantha Pecoraro
Cape Coral, Florida

"I suffer from something called eosinophilic esophagitis (EoE), which causes my body to think food is a parasite and attacks it," says 16-year-old Samantha Pecoraro, whose most passionate goal is to become a chef.

EoE causes an extreme reaction as a result of multiple food allergies. The disease has no cure and treatment comprises being fed a costly nutrition formula directly into a stomach port. Still, despite the fact that she can't even taste what she cooks, Samantha wants to make other people happy by creating delicious food. She got the chance when a D.C.-area chef, after hearing her story, invited her to cook alongside him in his restaurant for a few days. The end result of their efforts was a fundraising dinner for a foundation seeking a cure for EoE.

"I call myself The Blind Chef," she says. "Because when you are blind, your other senses are heightened. I feel that not being able to actually taste my food puts me in a similar situation. Because I can't taste food, my sense of smell has become a highly developed way to know how something will taste."

Since Samantha can't enjoy a meal with her family or a treat with friends, she spends her time out of the kitchen listening to music or reading the Bible. In addition to a future in cooking, Samantha's goal is to "one day to be able to taste the things I cook."

This **Sweet & Spicy Roast Chicken** is reminiscent of classic sweet and sour chicken preparations because of the vinegar base, but it's the taco sauce that gives it a dimension outside the ordinary. While jarred or canned taco sauce is readily available in most supermarkets, the extra effort to make your own is well worth the trouble for the depth it adds to the chicken. Samantha roasts her chicken, but this marinade makes it too good to not consider for the barbecue grill as well. If you choose to grill rather than roast the chicken, place the marinated pieces on a medium-hot grill and cook away over indirect heat for 15 to 20 minutes per side, or until cooked through, turning once. Baste frequently.

Serve the chicken with rice, Bacony Mac 'n' Cheese (page 102), or salad.

SWEET & SPICY ROAST CHICKEN   SERVES 4

½ cup Taco Sauce (recipe follows)

½ cup soy sauce

¼ cup honey

4 cloves garlic, minced

2 tablespoons light brown sugar

2 tablespoons sunflower oil

2 tablespoons cider vinegar

½ teaspoon finely minced fresh parsley

Salt and freshly ground black pepper

1 whole chicken (2 pounds), cut into 8 serving pieces

1. In a medium bowl, whisk together the taco sauce, soy sauce, honey, garlic, brown sugar, oil, vinegar, parsley, 2 teaspoons black pepper, and ⅛ teaspoon salt.

2. Wash the chicken pieces and pat dry. Season the chicken pieces with salt and pepper, then place the chicken in a baking dish.

3. Pour three-quarters of the marinade over the chicken pieces and cover the dish tightly with plastic wrap. Refrigerate the chicken overnight and reserve the remaining marinade.

4. Preheat the oven to 375°F.

5. Bake the chicken until a thermometer inserted into a leg piece reads 165°F, 45 minutes to 1 hour, brushing every 10 to 15 minutes with the remaining marinade.

Taco Sauce

   1 teaspoon sunflower oil
   1 tablespoon minced onion
   1 clove garlic, minced
   1 teaspoon tomato paste
   1 cup tomato puree
1¼ teaspoons salt
   1 teaspoon ground cumin
   ½ teaspoon dried epazote*
   ½ teaspoon cayenne pepper
   ¼ teaspoon smoked paprika
   ¼ teaspoon turmeric
   ¼ teaspoon brown sugar
   1 cup tomato sauce
   1 tablespoon apple cider vinegar

1. In a small saucepan, heat the oil over medium heat. Add the onion and garlic and cook, stirring often with a whisk, until the onion begins to soften and the garlic releases its aromas, 1 to 2 minutes. Do not allow the garlic to brown.

2. Add the tomato paste and tomato puree and cook, whisking, for 2 minutes more. Whisk in the salt, cumin, epazote, cayenne pepper, smoked paprika, turmeric, and brown sugar. Cook, stirring until the spices become fragrant, about 1 minute.

3. Add the tomato sauce, vinegar, and ¼ cup water, whisking so all the ingredients are well combined. Reduce the heat to a simmer and continue to cook the sauce until it is reduced by half and thickened, 10 to 15 minutes. Store unused taco sauce in an airtight container in the refrigerator.

*EPAZOTE *is a Mexican herb with a bright, aromatic flavor similar to fennel. It is most often used dried. Look for it in Latino or gourmet markets.*

Marshall Bennett
McLean, Virginia

Marshall Bennet started cooking when he was 9 as a way to help his then-pregnant mom. "I mixed some pasta wagon wheels, carrots, celery, chicken broth, and some spices that to this day I still can't name, and I made soup," he says.

From soup Marshall graduated to making flavored sunflower seeds when he was 11. Fusion is the theme of the seeds (as well as of his larger cooking) and some of the flavors, which he shares with his high school baseball team, included bacon and ranch, kung pao chicken, spicy chili, taco, steak, buffalo wing, and sweet and sour.

Because the teen most values the bonding opportunities that come with sharing his unique creations, he still continues the project he started as a fifth grader called the Chill Grille, a household delivery "restaurant" that he does for a limited set of weekends in the summer.

"I experiment for a few weeks with my own family, then we present a summer menu to the neighborhood," says the teen, who hopes one day to have a career in the United States Marine Corps. "I fix a set meal on a Friday night or a breakfast basket on a Saturday morning and families order which ones they want."

The effort earned him a feature in *Tocque* magazine in 2013. For now he's continuing to build bridges with even younger kids with his mashed-up explorations of world foods by sharing his sunflower seed mixes with the Little League team he coaches. "We really bond over those seeds," he says.

Grilled Caribbasian Citrus Chicken is the signature of Marshall's mashed-up cooking style in which, he says, "I like to combine dishes from wildly different cultures to make a single meal. I've mixed the sweet and sour of Asia with the fresh, exotic fruit of the Caribbean and called that menu 'Caribbasian,'" says Marshall, now 17. "And I love Italian food, so I tried mixing it with the Moroccan cuisine my mom loves and came up with 'Mo'Italian.'"

In this version, tropical flavor comes from citrus fruit and sweet heat of sugar and cayenne pepper. For an even more uniquely Caribbean feel, you may substitute $1/3$ cup mango, papaya, or guava juice for the orange juice. Serve with plain rice, Spring/Summer Vegetable Risotto (page 104), or Refreshing Thai Cucumber Salad (page 19).

GRILLED CARIBBASIAN CITRUS CHICKEN

SERVES 4

Juice of 1 orange

Juice of 1 lemon

1 tablespoon soy sauce

1 tablespoon white wine vinegar

¼ cup olive oil

¼ cup chopped fresh cilantro, plus more for garnish

⅛ teaspoon cayenne pepper (or more to taste)

Salt

2 pounds boneless, skinless chicken breasts, lightly pounded

2 tablespoons sugar

1. In a small bowl, whisk together the orange juice, lemon juice, soy sauce, white wine vinegar, olive oil, cilantro, cayenne, and ⅛ teaspoon salt.

2. Place the chicken in a large bowl and pour half the marinade over it. Mix well, cover tightly with plastic wrap, and refrigerate overnight. Refrigerate the reserved marinade separately.

3. Preheat a grill to high.

4. Add the chicken pieces and grill for 12 to 15 minutes per side.

5. While the chicken is grilling, strain the reserved marinade into a small saucepan and stir in the sugar and ¼ teaspoon salt. Bring to a simmer over medium-low heat and simmer until the sauce reduces by half, 6 to 8 minutes.

6. Drizzle the sauce on top of the grilled chicken and garnish with additional fresh cilantro.

Allie Cerruti
Modesto, California

Allie Cerruti never does anything halfway. A dedicated violinist who travels 1½ hours each direction to class and also takes lessons in drums and singing, she is also a member of a youth ballet company that makes school tours to teach other children about dance, and the self-styled Miss Junior Chef hosts a cooking website that is "for kids only," *Missjrchef.* While the audience is young, the recipes are far from childish, demonstrating Allie's interest in inclusive recipes. One of her goals is to brush up her repertoire to include dishes friendly to those suffering with diabetes. "Two of my best friends have this disease," she says. "I think it would be great to be able to make dishes for them that everyone enjoys."

Allie makes a straightforward version of Jerusalem chicken called **Creamy Chicken with Artichokes** that features heavy cream and artichoke hearts. It's important not to get artichoke hearts in brine or vinegar, which will make the final preparation too salty or sour. She suggests serving it with fettuccine, or simply on its own for those, like her friends, who need to avoid starch because of health concerns—for this purpose the wine may also be replaced with low-sodium chicken broth and 1 teaspoon of white wine vinegar.

CREAMY CHICKEN WITH ARTICHOKES (JERUSALEM CHICKEN)

SERVES 4

½ cup all-purpose flour

2 teaspoons salt

1 teaspoon freshly ground black pepper

2 pounds boneless, skinless chicken breasts, sliced into 1-inch strips

3 tablespoons olive oil

4 cloves garlic, minced

¼ cup minced shallots

1 can (14 ounces) water-packed artichoke hearts, drained and roughly chopped (or use frozen artichoke hearts)

1 cup white wine

2 cups heavy (whipping) cream

1. In a bowl, whisk together the flour, salt, and pepper.

2. Dredge the chicken strips in the flour mixture, shake of the excess, and place on a platter. Refrigerate for 15 minutes.

3. In a large skillet, heat the olive oil over medium heat. Drop a pinch of flour to test if it is ready. If the flour sizzles immediately the oil is hot enough. Working in batches if necessary, carefully add the chicken strips, taking care to not crowd them in the pan. Fry until lightly browned, 7 to 8 minutes per side. Turn only once.

4. Once the chicken looks golden brown, add the garlic, shallots, and artichokes and reduce the heat to medium-low. Cook the mixture for 3 to 5 minutes. Add the wine, increase the heat to medium, and cook until the wine is reduced by half, 5 to 7 minutes.

5. Stir in the cream. Let the mixture simmer until reduced by one-quarter, about 10 minutes. Serve hot.

Popy Aziz
Detroit, Michigan

Popy Aziz believes that food is identity and that people should know who you are just by looking at what you cook.

A member of the Detroit Food Academy, a local afterschool program that teaches cooking as a way to approach personal and community growth, Popy has used food as a way to teach others about her cultural and religious heritage by talking about the food proscriptions of her Islamic faith.

The most important Muslim holiday, Ramadan, presents an opportunity for Popy to express her culture through food. "My older sister and I stay up all night to cook different appetizers for the whole family for when we break our fast in the evening," says Popy of the month-long fasting holiday. "I come from a very colorful culture," the 16-year-old says about her Bangladeshi/Muslim heritage. "And that's going to help me create my own identity with food as I get older."

Popy's **Chicken 65** is an adaptation of a South Indian dish created in 1965 by a restaurant chef in the state of Tamil Nadu. Rice flour and cornstarch are integral to lending a crispy coating to the chicken and also make the dish gluten free. Patience is required in the last step of the process to ensure that the chicken pieces are not only well coated but retain their crispy texture. The spice list that makes up this dish is extensive, but the color of the final product and the most important informing flavor comes from the curry leaves, which should not be omitted. They are easily found in Indian and Middle Eastern markets.

CHICKEN 65

SERVES 4

Chicken

- 2 pounds boneless skinless chicken thighs, cut into 1-inch pieces
- ½ teaspoon turmeric
- ½ teaspoon red chile powder
- ¼ teaspoon freshly ground black pepper
- ½ teaspoon grated fresh ginger
- ½ teaspoon grated garlic
- ½ teaspoon lemon juice
- ½ teaspoon salt
- 1 egg
- 3 tablespoons cornstarch
- 2 tablespoons rice flour (available in Indian and Middle Eastern markets)
- 1 cup safflower oil

(continued)

Sauce

¾ cup nonfat plain yogurt

½ teaspoon salt

¼ teaspoon turmeric

¼ teaspoon red chile powder

¼ teaspoon ground coriander

1 tablespoon safflower oil

2 cloves garlic, minced

½ teaspoon minced fresh ginger

4 or 5 curry leaves (available in Indian and Middle Eastern markets)

2 small chile peppers, slit lengthwise
   Fresh cilantro leaves, for garnish
   Cooked rice, for serving

1. For the chicken: In a large bowl, season the chicken pieces with the turmeric, chile powder, black pepper, fresh ginger, garlic, lemon juice, and salt. Mix very well and set aside.

2. In a small bowl, beat the egg. In a second, shallow bowl, whisk together the cornstarch and rice flour.

3. Heat the oil in a large, deep skillet over medium heat for 2 minutes or until hot. Test the oil by dropping a pinch of flour into the oil, if it sizzles then it is ready.

4. Meanwhile, pour the egg over the chicken mixture and mix well so all the pieces are coated. Dip the chicken, a few pieces at a time, into the corn/rice flour mixture and toss well to coat. Repeat until all the pieces are coated.

5. Working in batches, add the chicken pieces to the pan in a single layer; do not crowd them in the pan. Fry until golden brown on all sides, 10 to 15 minutes. Remove chicken with a slotted spoon and place on a plate lined with paper towels.

6. For the sauce: In a medium bowl, whisk together the yogurt, salt, turmeric, chile powder, and coriander. Set aside.

7. Heat another large, deep skillet or saucepan over medium-low heat and add the oil. Add the garlic and ginger and sauté for a few seconds. Add the curry leaves and chiles and sauté for 30 seconds more. Add the deep-fried chicken, toss well and cook for 2 minutes.

8. Add the yogurt mixture to the chicken and cook on low to medium heat, mixing the contents well. Cook, tossing the chicken often until all the yogurt mixture is absorbed, 5 to 10 minutes.

9. Arrange on a platter and garnish with cilantro leaves. Serve with plain rice.

Jacob Shaik
Hinsdale, Illinois

"American allergy cuisine" is how Jacob Shaik, a 12-year-old from Illinois, describes his cooking. "I have many food allergies so I can't try a lot of the foods I'd like to try," says Jacob. "As a result I have to recreate recipes if I want to try them. Over time, I've learned how to use different ingredients, like olive oil instead of butter, and coconut milk instead of dairy milk, as well as coconut cream instead of yogurt or cream."

His love of cooking—and the need for specialty recipes—affords Jacob a special side benefit: spending more time with his mom. "I have three brothers, so spending quality time with her alone is special," says the tween. "We have fun recreating a dinner dish for my entire family to try." Jacob admits that cooking by substitution is not always "thumbs up," particularly in the dessert category, when you're not using milk, eggs, butter, or cream.

"Either way, my family and I have fun trying out new things or seeing the recipes improve each time I make them," he says. Jacob's filling for his **Chicken Pot Pie** has no butter or cream, depending instead on creamed corn and a flour paste to create thickness. While the shortening is mostly responsible for the flakiness in the crust, a tablespoon of solid olive oil (you freeze it to solidify) is added for flavor. For those seeking healthier fats, solid coconut oil is a good substitute for the shortening, but be aware that the crust, while tender, will not be quite as flaky.

Unlike a typical pot pie, this one features a larger variety of vegetables, and even spinach. In the spirit of experimentation, Jacob encourages other cooks to mix it up as well by considering substituting greens such as kale or bok choy in the mix, or other root vegetables such as parsnips. This dish is also lovely served as individual pot pies baked in small ramekins or baking dishes. Jacob's method calls for making the sauce in the same pot in which you browned the chicken—this means that the sauce in the pot pie will be browned and not white as is traditional. If you prefer a white pot pie sauce, heat the chicken broth in a separate pan and then add the flour paste and creamed corn.

(continued)

CHICKEN POT PIE

Dough

2½ cups all-purpose flour

1 teaspoon baking powder

1 teaspoon sugar

½ teaspoon salt

¼ teaspoon dried basil

¼ teaspoon dried oregano

⅛ teaspoon coarsely ground black pepper

1 tablespoon extra virgin olive oil, frozen

1 cup vegetable shortening, well chilled

½ cup ice water, or as needed

Filling

1½ pounds boneless, skinless chicken breast, cut into ½-inch chunks

1 teaspoon coarse salt

½ teaspoon garlic powder

½ teaspoon paprika

½ teaspoon freshly ground black pepper

2 tablespoons olive oil

¼ cup diced red bell pepper

¼ cup diced yellow or orange bell pepper

¼ cup diced yellow onion

2 cloves garlic, minced

1 teaspoon dried oregano

¼ teaspoon red pepper flakes

½ carrot, diced

½ celery stalk, diced

1 medium white potato, peeled and diced

¼ cup frozen chopped spinach, thawed and squeezed dry

¼ cup fresh or frozen green peas

¼ cup fresh or frozen corn kernels

2 cups fat-free low-sodium chicken broth

2 tablespoons flour mixed with 3 tablespoons water to form a creamy paste

¼ cup canned cream-style corn

2 tablespoons chiffonade of fresh basil (see page 116)

1. For the dough: In a medium bowl, whisk together the flour, baking powder, sugar, salt, basil, oregano, and pepper. Add the frozen olive oil and chilled vegetable shortening and, using a fork or pastry cutter, cut the shortening and oil into the flour mixture until it forms pea-size crumbs. (Alternatively, you can do this in a food processor by pulsing the flour mixture and shortening and oil together until it forms pea-size crumbs.)

2. Add the ice water in a slow stream while mixing until the mixture just comes together into a ball. (Or, pulsing the food processor on and off, pour the water in a slow stream through the feed tube.) Use more or less water as necessary to achieve this texture. Flatten the dough into a disk and then wrap the dough in plastic wrap and refrigerate for about 2 hours.

3. For the filling: Season the chicken with the salt, garlic powder, paprika, and black pepper. Heat a large skillet over medium heat and add 1 tablespoon of the olive oil. Heat the oil for 1 minute, then add enough chicken to fit comfortably in the pan, do not overcrowd the chicken. Cook the chicken in batches, if necessary. Cook the chicken for 7 to 8 minutes.

4. Remove the chicken with a slotted spoon and set aside in a large bowl. Add the remaining 1 tablespoon oil, and then the bell peppers and onion and sauté until the onion begins to soften, 3 to 5 minutes. Add the garlic, oregano, and pepper flakes and cook for 2 to 3 minutes, stirring often. Add

the carrot, celery, and potato, stir and sauté for 5 minutes. Add the spinach, peas, and corn and stir well. Cook for 1 minute more, then transfer the vegetables to the bowl with the chicken and set aside while you make the sauce.

5. Add the chicken broth to the skillet and bring to a boil. Stir in the flour mixture and whisk until well blended. When the mixture has begun to thicken, 1 to 2 minutes, stir in the creamed corn and fresh basil. Return the chicken and vegetables to the pan and stir well. Cook for 2 to 3 minutes more to combine flavors, then turn off the heat. Transfer to a 10-inch pie plate, 8 × 8-inch baking dish, or 6 individual ¾-cup ramekins.

6. Preheat the oven to 400°F.

7. Remove the chilled dough from the refrigerator and place the dough disk between 2 sheets of parchment paper. Roll out the dough to a round roughly 11 inches in diameter; or roll and cut out the crust to the appropriate size and shape for your chosen baking dish(es).

8. Carefully position the crust on top, tucking the edge inside the pie plate or baking dish(es). Pierce the crust in a few places to vent the steam while cooking.

9. Bake the pot pie(s) until the crust is golden brown and the sauce is bubbling, 30 to 40 minutes for a 10-inch pie and 20 to 25 minutes for individual ramekins. Let the pot pie(s) stand for 10 minutes before serving.

Francessca Ritchie
Blaine, Washington

The eldest of three sisters, 17-year-old Francessca Ritchie calls herself a traditional-yet-innovative cook who marries the spices and flavors of her native Trinidad to the ingredients locally available in Washington State where she now lives.

Often acting as the sous-chef for her mother Sarah's Caribbean cooking classes, Francessca began to seek ways to "lighten" up her dishes 4 years ago when her dad became ill with esophageal cancer and she and her sisters watched him go through chemotherapy, radiation, and surgery.

Part of the path Francessca laid out for herself and her sisters was to change all the ingredients they cooked with to organic, local, and wild for seafood. She's lightened up her family's curry chicken recipe by removing the chicken skin and suggests serving the chicken over brown rice instead of white rice as is traditionally done. **Trinidad Curry Chicken** calls for milder West Indian curry powder, so heat is added to the dish with a fresh Scotch bonnet pepper, the amount of which may seem small but still packs a powerful punch.

TRINIDAD CURRY CHICKEN

SERVES 4 TO 6

1 whole chicken (3 pounds), cut into 8 serving pieces, skin removed

Juice of 1 lime

2 teaspoons crushed garlic

1 cup chopped onions

1 cup chopped scallions

¼ Scotch bonnet pepper (or to taste), minced

4 sprigs fresh thyme

3 tablespoons finely chopped fresh cilantro

4 to 5 tablespoons West Indian curry powder (available in Caribbean markets)

½ cup hot water

2 tablespoons olive oil

1 teaspoon ground cumin

2 bay leaves

1 teaspoon salt

Freshly ground black pepper

Cooked brown or white rice, for serving

1. Place the chicken pieces in a large bowl, pour the lime juice over them, and mix well. Drain the lime juice, pat the chicken dry with paper towels, and return to the bowl.

2. Add the garlic, onions, scallions, Scotch bonnet pepper, thyme, and cilantro to the chicken and mix well. Cover with plastic wrap and marinate in the refrigerator for at least 1 hour and up to 4 hours.

3. In a small bowl, mix the curry powder with the hot water to form a thick paste.

4. In a large deep pot, heat the olive oil over medium heat. Add the curry paste and cook, stirring constantly, until the paste loses its grainy appearance, about 2 minutes. Stir in the cumin and cook 1 minute more.

5. Add the chicken pieces with their marinade and mix well so that every piece of chicken is coated with the curry mixture. Add 2 cups water or just enough to barely cover the chicken and add the bay leaves, salt, and black pepper to taste. Reduce the heat to medium-low and simmer the curry, uncovered, until the chicken removes easily from the bone with a fork, about 45 minutes. Discard the bay leaves. Serve with brown or white rice.

Charles Alan Welch
Richmond, Virginia

The re-enactment cooks at the Governor's Palace in Colonial Williamsburg first noticed 14-year-old Alan Welch quietly hanging around the kitchens as they cooked—sometimes for whole mornings at a time. Eventually the young man started asking questions about their methods and about 18th-century cooking in general and it became clear that his passion for historic foodways was more than a passing interest. "I've loved cooking since my parents took down the child safety gate to our kitchen and let me in to watch them cook," he says. The home-schooled teen says he's always loved history so when he first saw the cooking re-enactments at Colonial Williamsburg he was mesmerized, and the more he researched the era the more fascinated he became.

Alan and his mom, Tammy, both native Virginians, have travelled to historic sites far and wide just to get a peek at an 18th-century kitchen, but Alan gets to indulge his passion closer to home every Wednesday when he visits Colonial Williamsburg to practice with the Fifes and Drums of Yorktown, in which he plays the bass drum.

The group has performed at historic sites such as George Washington's Mt. Vernon and Yorktown itself. When he's not visiting a historic site, Alan, is working on a school project about breads of the 1700s and cooking his way through the recipes on *History Is Served*, the cooking blog of the Colonial Williamsburg Foundation. "My goal is to go to culinary school and then apprentice in the Historic Foodways department at the restoration," he says. "To be a cooking interpreter at Colonial Williamsburg—that would be a dream come true."

Alan's **Colonial-Cola Pot Roast** is adapted from a family favorite made by his grandmother. In it, he uses a Dutch oven, one of the most common 18th-century cooking utensils, along with a full complement of the warm spices of cinnamon, nutmeg, and cloves that were popular in early American kitchens for savory dishes as well as sweet. The pairing of these flavors with citrus, such as the orange in this recipe, was common as well. The addition of cola—a 20th-century Southern technique—similar flavor notes and enhances the body of the pot roast. This roast pairs well with a good rustic bread or egg noodles prepared according to package directions.

COLONIAL-COLA POT ROAST

SERVES 6 TO 8

2 tablespoons butter

2 medium yellow onions, thinly sliced

4 carrots, cut into 1-inch pieces

1 turnip, cut into 1-inch chunks

1 orange, thinly sliced

3 pound boneless chuck roast, trimmed of external fat

Salt and freshly ground black pepper

3 cloves garlic, thinly sliced

2 tablespoons dried onion

2 teaspoons dark brown sugar

½ teaspoon ground cinnamon

½ teaspoon paprika

⅛ teaspoon ground cloves

⅛ teaspoon freshly grated nutmeg

2 cups beef broth

2 cups cola

4 sprigs fresh thyme

1. Preheat the oven to 325°F.

2. In a large skillet, melt 1 tablespoon of the butter over medium heat. Add half the onions and sauté until softened and translucent, 3 to 4 minutes.

3. In a large Dutch oven or other deep ovenproof casserole, layer the carrots, turnip, the remaining half of the onions, and half the orange slices. Season the roast well with salt and pepper and then place on top of the vegetables in the pan.

4. In a large saucepan, melt the remaining 1 tablespoon butter over medium heat. Add the garlic slices and cook 1 minute. Add the dried onion and brown sugar and stir until the sugar begins to melt. Add the cinnamon, paprika, cloves, nutmeg, 1 teaspoon salt, and ½ teaspoon black pepper and mix well. Gently pour in the beef broth and cola and stir well.

5. Pour the spiced cola mixture over the beef in the Dutch oven. Layer the remaining sautéed onions on top of the roast and the sliced oranges on top of that. Add the thyme to the pot, cover, and bake for 1 hour 30 minutes. Uncover and bake until a thermometer inserted into the center of the roast reads 160°F, about 1 hour 30 minutes longer. Serve, sliced, with the vegetables.

Jonathan Marin
Norwood, New Jersey

Bullied by students and even teachers who did not understand his condition, 11-year-old Jonathan Marin, who has Asperger syndrome, left school for the shelter and solitude of home. While his mother, Victoria, home-schooled her son, Jonathan found an outlet for his feelings in the ballroom and the kitchen.

"I was very hurt and felt bad about myself," says the now 13-year-old Jonathan. "I started to take ballroom dance lessons. Dancing helped me to feel better. It helped me to have more confidence so that I was not afraid of getting made fun of if I made mistakes." At the same time, cooking gave Jonathan a way to show warmth and love to others—feelings that are not easily demonstrated by those with Asperger syndrome.

"I believe that food touches the soul of everybody. Food is comforting," says Jonathan, who, at 10, created 4-spice roasted chicken to donate to the local soup kitchen supported by his church. Now a student at a local culinary studio, Jonathan plans out entire meals for his family, including those for special holidays.

While he prefers the solitude of cooking alone, sharing his cuisine with others has allowed him to experience the intersection of food and feeling. More than anything, says Jonathan, cooking has taught him there are ways to feel good about oneself even when things get hard. "I feel like I can be proud of myself when I cook. I want other children like me to know that there are ways out there to help them feel good even after they have been bullied."

Jonathan's **Marinated Skirt Steak** is marinated in a combination of balsamic vinegar, Worcestershire sauce, aromatics, and spices. The intensity of the sauce allows the meat to have a relatively short marinating time—only a few hours versus overnight. For best results, allow excess marinade to drain off the steak before grilling. If you are especially fond of onion flavor you can even go so far as to grate the onion rather than mince it, which will release more of the pungent onion juice into the marinade. Once the steak is finished cooking, be generous with the freshly chopped parsley garnish—it adds a fresh flavor dimension that complements the well-seasoned meat. Serve with Jonathan's Baked Beans (page 83).

MARINATED SKIRT STEAK

½ cup balsamic vinegar

½ cup vegetable oil

¼ cup Worcestershire sauce

1 small onion, finely chopped

1 tablespoon minced garlic

1 tablespoon cayenne pepper

1 tablespoon ground cumin

1 tablespoon paprika

1 teaspoon freshly ground black pepper

4 pound skirt steak

   Freshly chopped parsley, for garnish

1. In a large bowl, whisk together the vinegar, oil, and Worcestershire sauce. Add the onion, garlic, cayenne, cumin, paprika, and black pepper. Whisk well.

2. Place the skirt steak in a large deep platter or marinating container and pour the marinade over it. A large zip-top bag works well for this purpose too. Marinate the steak in the refrigerator for 2 to 3 hours.

3. Preheat a grill to high. Sear the skirt steak 5 to 6 minutes on each side. Do not overcook or the skirt steak will be tough. Remove from heat and allow to rest for 2 to 3 minutes and then slice into ½-inch slices for serving.

Teddy Devico
Warren, New Jersey

Empathy has been one of the primary motivators in the cooking life of Teddy Devico, an 18-year-old who is now in his freshman year at Cornell's School of Hotel Administration. "I have severe food allergies. I never have been, and most likely never will be, able to eat fish, nuts, or seeds," he says. "As a passionate 'foodie,' it is frustrating to never have tried sushi and other dishes that are so well liked."

Because of his allergies, Teddy understands a thing or two about limitations, so he was more than happy to lend a hand, first as a cook and then as an organizer, for the Autism Speaks fundraiser in his town.

"I spent most every day after school my junior year speaking to sponsors, advertising the event, or devising the menu," says Teddy. Ultimately, the fundraiser went off without a hitch, raising $1,500 for the organization.

Teddy says his favorite part of cooking is the chance not only to help others but to be artistic as well. "My favorite aspect of working with food is the creativity," he says. "In most other ways I am not that artistic or creative. However, in the kitchen I feel that I can be creative and come up with different flavor and textural combinations that are usually successful."

The **Beef Brisket** that Teddy prepares makes use of tart Granny Smith apples to balance the sweetness of caramelized carrots, parsnips, and honey. The apple flavor is upped by both apple juice and apple cider vinegar, and another acidic dimension comes from red wine.

Use a good-quality dry red wine that is crisp enough to marry with the fattiness of the meat and the sweetness of the aromatics. French Burgundy or Pinot Noir are good choices.

BEEF BRISKET

2½ pounds beef brisket

Salt and freshly ground black pepper

1 teaspoon safflower oil

2 carrots, roughly chopped

1 parsnip, roughly chopped

1 turnip, roughly chopped

8 cloves garlic, crushed through a press

4 large onions, thinly sliced

2 Granny Smith apples, cored and roughly chopped

2 cups dry red wine

1 cup apple cider vinegar

1 cup apple juice

¼ cup honey

2 bay leaves

1 teaspoon chopped fresh thyme

1 teaspoon chopped fresh rosemary

1. Preheat the oven to 300°F.

2. Dry off the brisket with paper towels and season liberally with salt and pepper. Heat a large skillet over medium heat and add the safflower oil. Add the brisket and sear 8 minutes per side or until browned on all sides. Remove the brisket from the pan and drain off most of the fat that has rendered from the meat, leaving 1 tablespoon of fat in the pan.

3. Add the carrots, parsnip, turnip, garlic, onions, and apples. Season with salt and pepper to taste and mix well. Cook the vegetables over medium-low until the apple pieces begin to caramelize, 6 to 8 minutes.

4. Add the wine to the vegetables and bring to a boil, then reduce the heat to a simmer and add the vinegar, apple juice, honey, bay leaves, thyme, and rosemary. Return the brisket to the pot, cover, and bake until the brisket is easily pierced with a fork and a thermometer reads 160°F, 3 to 4 hours.

5. Remove the brisket and set aside to rest. Discard the bay leaves. Scoop the vegetables out of the pot and set aside.

6. Place the pot over medium heat and simmer until the liquid is reduced enough to coat the back of a spoon, 10 to 15 minutes.

7. Meanwhile, preheat the oven to broil.

8. Slice the brisket into 1-inch slices and arrange in a broilerproof baking dish with the cooked vegetables. Drizzle with the reduced sauce and broil for 10 minutes to brown slightly.

Sydney Michael Brown
Fuquay-Varina, North Carolina

Sharing her culinary gifts to uplift others is part of Healthy Lunchtime Challenge winner Sydney Brown's long-term plan (see more on page 93). "When I become an adult and finish college, my goal is to own my own restaurant," says the 12-year-old self-described traditional Southern cook.

"I want my restaurant to be a place that people come and the food touches their hearts and takes them on a journey to a familiar place, like home or a favorite vacation," she says. "To have food in my life gives me joy, and to have my own restaurant will give me the chance to show it."

Sydney's **Homerun Meat Loaf Burger** is a twist on the down-home meat loaf she learned in her mother's, grandmother's, and great-grandmother's kitchens. It features a wealth of chopped fresh vegetables for both flavor and nutritional purposes in a new-yet-familiar dish to harken happy memories of home. The burgers are equally good on a bun or on their own with a side salad for a lighter meal. They're also good with her Zucchini Fries (page 71).

HOMERUN MEAT LOAF BURGER SERVES 8

2 pounds lean ground beef

½ cup finely diced green bell pepper

½ cup finely diced zucchini

½ cup finely diced onion

½ cup plain dried breadcrumbs

1 clove garlic, minced

1 egg

Salt and freshly ground black pepper

½ cup ketchup

½ cup barbecue sauce

8 slices reduced-fat provolone cheese (or any other type of reduced-fat melting cheese), if desired

8 whole wheat or multigrain hamburger buns, split and toasted

Lettuce and tomato, for garnish

1. Preheat the oven to 425°F. Line a baking sheet with parchment paper or coat with cooking spray.

2. In a large bowl, mix together the ground beef, bell pepper, zucchini, onion, breadcrumbs, garlic, egg, and salt and black pepper to taste. Form into 8 patties and place them on the baking sheet.

3. Bake for about 10 minutes and then flip them and bake for another 10 minutes.

4. In a small bowl, mix together the ketchup and barbecue sauce and brush on each of the burgers, then bake for an additional 10 to 15 minutes.

5. Add a slice of cheese to each burger, if using, and bake until melted, about 1 minute.

6. To serve, place the burgers on the buns and garnish with lettuce and tomato.

Jack Witherspoon
Redondo Beach, California

John Hansen Witherspoon, known as Jack, first came to cooking while housebound from treatment for leukemia when he was 5 years old. Food Network, he says, was his constant companion, and when he was well enough, he was able to get into the kitchen and try his hand at cooking. Jack came to consider himself a cook when, at 7 years old, he hosted his own fundraiser for pediatric leukemia research in 2007, creating his own menu and recipes (with the help of some professional chefs) for a 300-person event.

"Being a kid, I may not have the culinary experience of an 'adult' cook, but I guess that's one reason why I haven't fallen into any bad habits or cooking ruts," says Jack, who is now 13. "I love experimenting with new ingredients. The more I learn about food and cooking, the more I realize how much more there is to know."

That ever-curious attitude has allowed Jack to perfect his craft enough to release his own mass-market cookbook, *Twist It Up,* in 2011 and in 2013 he was a contestant on *Rachael vs. Guy* on Food Network. He's also appeared on *The Tonight Show* and others. The now three-time leukemia survivor has used his skills and celebrity to raise more than $150,000 for pediatric leukemia research and has established his own endowment at Miller Children's Hospital in Long Beach, California.

Owning his own restaurant is at the top of the eighth grader's dream list for when he grows up, but, he says, that has to go hand-in-hand with continuing to raise money to find a cure for pediatric leukemia. "It's important to find a cure so other kids won't have to go through what I have had to," he says.

Jack's signature dish is the **Shepherd's Pie** he developed when he was 8 years old and that he demonstrated on *The Tonight Show* with host Jay Leno acting as sous-chef.

Jack's recipe calls for cubed beef roast, which harkens back to the original English version of this dish, called "cottage pie," while ground beef has become the American standard. The potato topping should not be an afterthought but a layer of equal importance, so the young cook has developed a fluffy, garlic-infused mashed potato that smoothes easily over the top of the meat filling. For a more elegant look, fit a pastry bag with a large star tip, fill with the mashed potato mixture, and pipe it in dollops over the top of the pie.

(continued)

SHEPHERD'S PIE

Filling

½ cup all-purpose flour

1 teaspoon garlic powder

Salt and freshly ground black pepper

1¼ pounds beef rib-eye roast, cut into 1-inch cubes

1 tablespoon olive oil

½ cup chopped yellow onion

½ cup chopped carrot

3 cloves garlic, minced

¾ cup beef broth

½ cup chopped tomatoes

2 teaspoons sugar

1½ teaspoons minced fresh thyme

½ cup frozen peas

Mashed potato topping

3 large russet (baking) potatoes, peeled and diced

2 teaspoons salt

4 tablespoons (½ stick) unsalted butter, at room temperature

⅛ teaspoon freshly grated nutmeg

¾ cup milk, at room temperature, or more as needed

3 cloves Roasted Garlic (recipe follows)

1. For the filling: In a deep dish, whisk together the flour, garlic powder, ½ teaspoon salt, and pepper. Dredge the beef pieces in the flour mixture so that it is coated on all sides. Shake off the excess.

2. In a large, heavy saucepan, heat the olive oil over medium-high heat. Add the onion and carrot and cook until the onion begins to soften, 3 to 4 minutes. Add the beef pieces to the saucepan and cook until browned on all sides, 8 to 9 minutes. Add the garlic and sauté for 1 minute, then add the beef broth, tomatoes, sugar, and thyme. Stir well. Bring to a boil, then reduce the heat to a simmer, cover, and cook until the carrots are just tender and the gravy is thickened and bubbling, 25 to 30 minutes. Stir in the peas and season with salt and pepper to taste.

3. For the mashed potato topping: Put the potatoes in a large pot with enough cold water to cover the potatoes by 3 inches. Add the salt and bring to a boil. Cook until tender, 15 to 20 minutes. Drain well and return the potatoes to the pot. Cook, shaking the pan, over medium heat for 30 seconds or so to cook off the excess water.

4. Preheat the oven to 375°F.

5. Add the butter and nutmeg to the potatoes and mash with a potato masher. Using an electric mixer, gradually beat in the milk and roasted garlic until smooth and fluffy. You may add more milk for fluffier potatoes.

(continued)

6. Spoon the beef mixture into a 9½-inch deep-dish pie plate or an 8 × 8-inch baking dish. Spoon the mashed potatoes on top and smooth evenly with a spatula. You may then use a fork to create tracks or a pattern in the potatoes.

7. Bake the pie for 15 minutes. In the last 5 minutes of cooking, place the pie on the top rack of the oven, right below the heat element so that the potatoes begin to brown. Remove from the oven and allow the pie to cool for 5 to 10 minutes before serving.

Roasted Garlic

MAKES 2 GARLIC HEADS

Slow-roasting whole heads of garlic is a wonderful method for intensifying the bulb's sweetness while cooking out the acridity that garlic may sometimes have. Whole roasted garlic cloves can keep for up to 1 week refrigerated, and are useful to have on hand to add to dishes that could use the best of the garlic but not the bitter. Use roasted garlic in mashed potatoes, dips, or by itself as a spread.

2 large heads garlic
2 teaspoons extra virgin olive oil

1. Preheat the oven to 350°F.
2. Slice about ⅛ inch off the top of each garlic head so that the tips of all of the cloves are exposed. Place each garlic head on a square of foil that is large enough to fold up and around the garlic head. Drizzle each garlic head with 1 teaspoon olive oil and 1 tablespoon water.

3. Bake until the garlic is caramelized and tender, about 30 minutes. Remove from the oven, open the foil packets and allow to cool. Store wrapped in the refrigerator for up to 1 week.

Logan Guleff
Memphis, Tennessee

Little did 12-year-old Logan Guleff know that stirring up coffee for his mama when he was 3 years old would eventually land him a meeting with the President of the United States when he was 10. Logan, the Tennessee winner of the Healthy Lunchtime Challenge, says he started out just loving to mix anything and everything—a pastime that led him to his passion for mixing together new flavors.

"I love to go get spices and try mixing my own blends. For example, the subtle flavors of different types of salt really intrigue me," says Logan, whose tuna quinoa salad got him invited to the White House for the Kids' "State Dinner". But even after the thrill of meeting President Obama and First Lady Michelle Obama, Logan still gets the biggest kick watching others enjoy his food at the local soup kitchen where he helps out.

"I love going and working there," he says, "I really think the most exciting part of cooking is when you serve your food and people love it. That can be a great feeling."

In the summer of 2013, Logan became the youngest person to take and pass a judging class in order to be a Memphis barbecue competition judge. Grilling and barbecue is the culinary technique that excites Logan most. His **Mediterranean Pork** was born of his love of taking a risk with taste. "I just put together the flavors I love best," he says referring to olives, feta cheese, and rosemary. "I made this marinade for grilled pork—it was risky but the finished product was just so good and really unexpected."

The key to this marinade is to pulse the ingredients in a food processor or blender until they are fairly smooth so that all the flavors are well incorporated and evenly distributed.

(continued)

MEDITERRANEAN PORK

¼ cup pitted Cerignola olives or other good-quality green olives (not canned)

¼ cup pitted kalamata olives or other good-quality black olives (not canned)

½ cup feta cheese cubes in olive oil, drained

½ head Roasted Garlic (page 166)

   Leaves from 5 sprigs fresh flat-leaf parsley

¼ cup extra virgin olive oil

1 small sprig fresh rosemary

   Salt and freshly ground black pepper

3 to 4 pounds pork loin

1. In a food processor, combine the olives, feta cheese, roasted garlic, and parsley and pulse until you have a coarse paste. Add the olive oil, rosemary, and pepper to taste and continue to pulse until you have a loose paste.

2. Season the pork with salt and pepper and place it in a deep dish. Spread half of the olive mixture all over the pork loin and cover the dish tightly with plastic wrap. Refrigerate for 2 to 3 hours. Set the reserved marinade aside.

3. Preheat a grill to high (about 450°F).

4. Place the tenderloin on the grill and cook for 7 to 8 minutes. Flip the pork over and grill until a thermometer inserted in the middle of the loin reads 140°F, 6 to 7 minutes. While it cooks, brush the reserved marinade on the loin at intervals, using all the marinade. The finished loin will have a slightly crispy crust.

5. If using a gas grill, turn off the heat, lower the lid, and let the loin sit in the grill for 5 more minutes. If using a charcoal grill, move the loin away from the direct heat and cook 3 to 4 minutes more.

6. Remove the pork loin from the grill and allow to rest for 10 to 15 min before slicing thinly to serve.

Randy McKinney
Meriden, Connecticut

Randy McKinney's mom figured he was the best kid for the job of helping out while she worked, so it was up to him to make lunch for his seven brothers and three sisters ages 9 to 22. Randy, who is now 17, has carried that spirit of caring for others from his home into the world. He volunteers at the Women & Families Center in his hometown of Meriden and works at Meriden Youth Services Center as a teen researcher—a group of young people who research ways to effect positive change in their communities. He also volunteers at the LGBT youth group in town because "I understand that people in general can struggle to fit in and gay people can have an even harder time," he says. "I volunteer to try to help them feel better and know they have a friend who knows what they went through."

When he was 15 years old, he joined My City Kitchen, another local nonprofit dedicated to helping kids build healthy habits and personal esteem through learning to cook. The chance to work with other kids and to exercise his love of math and method through cooking led Randy to stay with the program for more than 2 years, moving up in the ranks to an assistant teen chef for founder Chef Kashia Cave.

While the teen cooks international foods that he has learned at My City Kitchen, he still counts the foods of his Hispanic heritage to be his specialty. He makes **Pernil**, the classic Puerto Rican roast pork, for his family for holidays and special events.

Adobo seasoning and sofrito are classic Puerto Rican mixtures that give these dishes flavor. The former is a mix of dry spices and the latter is a seasoning paste of herbs and aromatic vegetables. Both are readily available premade, but your *pernil* will taste much better if you take the extra time and make these seasoning stars yourself. The extra can be used to add a little zest to roast chicken as well.

Serve the *pernil* with roasted potatoes or rice.

PERNIL

½ cup Adobo Seasoning (page 65)

1 tablespoon garlic powder

1 tablespoon paprika

2 teaspoons ground cumin

2 teaspoons salt

½ teaspoon ground coriander

½ teaspoon freshly ground black pepper

½ cup extra virgin olive oil

2 tablespoons Sofrito (recipe follows)

3 to 4 pounds boneless pork shoulder

1. Preheat the oven to 350°F.

2. In a medium bowl, whisk together the adobo seasoning, garlic powder, paprika, cumin, salt, coriander, and black pepper. Stir in the olive oil and sofrito.

3. Place the pork shoulder in a baking dish or roasting pan fat-side down. Using, a small, sharp paring knife, cut small slits all around the meat on all sides. Rub the spice mixture into the pork shoulder, stuffing the mixture into the slits in the meat.

4. Cover the pan with foil and bake until a thermometer inserted in the middle of the roast reads 165°F, 3 to 4 hours. Remove the foil for the last 30 minutes of cooking, basting every 10 minutes with the drippings.

Sofrito

MAKES 1 CUP

This seasoning paste is often considered the most important building block of Puerto Rican cuisine. Whether used as a rub on roasting meats or sautéed in oil as a precursor to stews and soups, this all-purpose mixture is a standard condiment in the Puerto Rican kitchen that can add flavor to a variety of non-Latino soups, stews and roasted and grilled meats as well. Consider using sofrito as a seasoning paste on your next Thanksgiving turkey.

3 to 4 ají dulce peppers

3 medium cubanelle peppers, seeded

1 large onion, roughly chopped

1 head garlic, separated into cloves and peeled

1 bunch of Mexican culantro or cilantro

1 bunch of parsley, stemmed

Combine all the ingredients in a food processor and process until smooth. Sofrito may be stored, refrigerated, for up to 2 weeks.

Wes Beeler
Westport, Connecticut

Every summer 14-year-old Wes Beeler competes in the Kansas City–sanctioned Blues Views & BBQ Festival contest in his hometown of Westport, an event, he says, that has pushed him to be at the top of his game. "There is no preparation allowed before the contest starts, like brining, marinating, or dry-rubbing the meat," he says. "That means you have to do all you can to make the flavor the best it can be, right at the grill."

The eighth grader, who started competing when he was 10 and earned third place in the Chef's Choice section of the competition in 2011, says his biggest influence is his dad, who is not only the primary cook at home but also worked as a chef through college and after. Wes has taken on more responsibility as sous-chef since his father became a vegetarian 4 years ago, "It's become my job to taste the meat-based dishes and suggest additions or changes," says the teen, who counts a church-mission trip to help renovate the homes of underprivileged families in Kentucky as an influential life event, for both ethical and culinary reasons.

"I enjoyed seeing all the cultural differences but especially the local food like biscuits and gravy—which I had for breakfast almost every morning," he says.

Wes shares his **Competition-Ready St. Louis-Style Spareribs** recipe here. Admittedly, this multilayered recipe is rather complex, but every step in the process is designed to enhance and deepen the flavor of the ribs. Low and slow is key to impart the sweet and smoky flavor note of the ribs, so patience is an unwritten ingredient that you'll need in abundance. Cayenne and Picka-peppa hot sauce figure prominently in either the dry rub or wet marinade on the ribs, and while you can certainly reduce their amounts if you don't care for spice, you'll find that the mellowing property of the smoke morphs their pure heat into a warming, aromatic accent.

GF

COMPETITION-READY ST. LOUIS–STYLE SPARERIBS

SERVES 4 TO 6

Dry rub

¾ cup dark brown sugar

¾ cup paprika

¼ cup salt

1 tablespoon freshly ground black pepper

1 tablespoon ground white pepper

1 tablespoon cayenne pepper

2 tablespoons garlic powder

2 tablespoons onion powder

2 tablespoons mustard powder

½ teaspoon celery seeds

½ teaspoon freshly ground black pepper

½ teaspoon ground white pepper

½ teaspoon cayenne pepper

1 tablespoon garlic powder

Salt

Ribs

3 slabs of St. Louis–cut spareribs

Hardwood charcoal (about 10 pounds)

Hickory wood chunks (about 4 pounds)

1 cup apple cider vinegar

¼ cup brown sugar

BBQ sauce

¼ cup olive oil

½ cup chopped celery

¼ cup chopped onion

¾ cup tomato paste

¾ cup distilled white vinegar

¼ cup maple syrup

2 tablespoons Pickapeppa sauce

1 tablespoon smoked paprika

1. For the dry rub: In a medium bowl whisk together the brown sugar, paprika, salt, black pepper, white pepper, cayenne, garlic powder, onion powder, and dry mustard.

2. For the ribs: Remove the membrane from the inside of the ribs then thoroughly rub ribs with enough dry rub until they are coated on all sides. Refrigerate overnight. Extra rub may be stored in an airtight container for up 1 month.

3. Set up a charcoal grill or smoker for indirect cooking using hardwood charcoal. When the coals are glowing, add the hickory chunks and additional charcoal to bring the grill up to an internal temperature of 220°F. After the flame created by the addition of the hickory and charcoal begins to subside, adjust the grill vents and/or add additional charcoal to maintain the temperature. At this point, the grill is ready.

(continued)

4. Combine the cider vinegar and brown sugar in a spray bottle and shake very well until the sugar dissolves. Spray the coal pile lightly with this mixture, as needed, to maintain a constant level of smoke. You do not want the wood to burn too quickly. The interior of the grill or smoker should maintain a constant temperature of 220°F.

5. Put the ribs on the smoker over indirect heat (not directly above the coals). Close the grill or smoker lid and allow the coals to smolder. Occasionally lift the lid and spray the coals with the cider mixture as needed to maintain the temperature; add additional charcoal or hickory as needed. Smoke the ribs for 4 to 5 hours or until a thermometer inserted into the meaty part of the ribs reads 165° to 170°F.

6. Meanwhile, for the barbecue sauce: In a heavy saucepan, heat the oil over medium heat. Add the celery and onion and cook until soft, 4 to 5 minutes. Do not brown. Add 1 cup water, the tomato paste, vinegar, maple syrup, Pickapeppa sauce, smoked paprika, celery seeds, black pepper, white pepper, cayenne, garlic powder, and salt to taste. Whisk well to combine and reduce the heat to a simmer. Cook this mixture until reduced by one-third, about 45 minutes.

7. Pour the sauce into a blender and puree into a smooth thick sauce.

8. Fifteen minutes before the ribs are done, remove them from the heat and place them on sheets of heavy-duty foil that are large enough to enfold the ribs completely. Paint the ribs with the BBQ sauce and wrap them in the foil. Return the wrapped ribs to the smoker for 15 minutes.

9. Serve with BBQ sauce on the side for dipping.

Georgianna Ritchie
Blaine, Washington

The middle sister in a trio of cooking siblings, Georgianna Ritchie says she'll try anything once—as long as it includes meat. Part of Georgianna's Girl vs. Food approach to cooking is, she says, never getting intimidated by the ingredients.

"I go for it, I use whatever ingredients that are available and make it work for whatever I'm trying to cook," says the 14-year-old. "I am also not afraid of hot peppers. I use them abundantly to my stomach's demise." Georgianna's **Spicy Italian Sausage & Spinach Frittata** came about using whatever was available in the kitchen—along with the fact, she says, that she can never just make "plain eggs." While she douses hers with hot pepper sauce, you can omit if desired.

SPICY ITALIAN SAUSAGE & SPINACH FRITTATA

SERVES 4

4 large eggs

¼ cup whole milk

2 teaspoons olive oil

1 small onion, finely chopped

2 hot Italian sausage patties (about 8 ounces), minced

½ red bell pepper, cut into ¼-inch-wide strips

2 cups roughly chopped fresh spinach

Salt and freshly ground black pepper

2 teaspoons butter

3 scallions, finely chopped

Hot pepper sauce

Crusty bread, for serving

1. Preheat the oven to 350°F.

2. In a medium bowl, beat together the eggs and milk. Set aside.

3. In a large cast-iron skillet, heat the oil over medium heat. Add the onions and sauté until they are soft and translucent, 3 to 4 minutes. Add the sausage and bell pepper and cook until the sausage begins to brown lightly, 5 to 6 minutes. Add the spinach and salt and pepper to taste. Cook until the spinach wilts, 2 to 3 minutes. Remove the sausage mixture from the pan and set aside.

4. Add the butter to the pan and add the scallions. Sauté the scallions for 1 minute, then add the egg mixture. Reduce the heat to medium-low. As the egg mixture firms up, gently push the edges in toward the center of the pan. Tilt the pan so the uncooked eggs run out to the edges to firm.

5. Add the sausage mixture to the middle of the egg mixture, spreading it out evenly. Place in the oven and bake until it firms up, 5 to 6 minutes. Do not let it overbrown.

6. Cut into 4 wedges. Serve garnished with hot sauce to taste and crusty bread on the side.

Hunter Zampa
Stamford, Connecticut

"I-Thai" is how Hunter Zampa refers to his cooking style, which is a mixture of his Italian-American grandmother's recipes and the Thai food that he personally loves. Thirteen-year-old Hunter, who has been a contestant on both the teen edition of *Chopped* and *Rachael vs. Guy* on Food Network, says his life-goal is to become an Iron Chef. "To be an Iron Chef would define me," he says.

Because he believes that cooking can change anyone's life as it has his, Hunter volunteers in the kitchen at the Boys and Girls Club in his hometown of Stamford, Connecticut. As a project preceding his Bar Mitzvah ceremony this year, during which the teen was formally accepted into the Jewish faith of his mother's family, Hunter collected donated utensils and other cooking necessities for the Boys and Girls Club kitchen. "My goal is to help every kid to cook—no matter who they are," he says.

When he's cooking at home, Hunter applies his "I-Thai" cooking style to whatever's at hand, especially the game meats his father, an avid hunter, brings home—as in this **Venison Medallions with Peanut Sauce.** "The peanut sauce is sweet, spicy, sour, and salty; and balances perfectly with the lean yet flavorful seared venison," he says.

Serve the venison with roasted potatoes and Refreshing Thai Cucumber Salad (page 19).

VENISON MEDALLIONS WITH PEANUT SAUCE

SERVES 4 TO 6

Peanut sauce

½ cup soy sauce

¼ cup Thai fish sauce

¼ cup lemon juice

2 teaspoons minced fresh ginger

1 teaspoon ground cardamom

1 teaspoon ground coriander

1 teaspoon ground cumin

1 teaspoon red pepper flakes

½ cup brown sugar

1 teaspoon toasted sesame oil

¾ cup creamy peanut butter

Venison medallions

Salt and freshly ground black pepper

2 pounds venison backstrap or tenderloin

1 teaspoon safflower oil

Sesame seeds

1. For the peanut sauce: In a small saucepan, whisk together the soy sauce, fish sauce, lemon juice, ginger, cardamom, coriander, cumin, and pepper flakes. Stir in the brown sugar and simmer over medium-low heat, stirring until the sugar melts. Add the sesame oil and peanut butter and continue to whisk until the peanut butter melts and you have a smooth sauce. Remove from the heat.

2. For the venison medallions: Season the venison generously with salt and pepper.

3. Heat a large skillet over medium heat and add the oil. Add the venison and sear on all sides, until the meat is cooked to medium-rare and a thermometer inserted into the thickest part reads 135°F, 15 to 18 minutes.

4. Remove the venison from the pan and allow to rest for 10 minutes. Slice the loin into ½-inch medallions and layer on a platter. Drizzle with the peanut sauce (if the peanut sauce was made ahead, warm it first over low heat). Garnish the medallions with sesame seeds.

CHAPTER 6

On the Rise

(Bread/Muffins/Rolls)

In the hands of these young chefs, breads, rolls, and muffins morph from being the simple staff of life into a kaleidoscope of form and flavor. The recipes in this section demonstrate their comfort with everything from yeast-based breads and complex laminate dough like that used for croissants, all the way to simple crackers and a gluten-free option as well. More than anything, though, what the breads in this section demonstrate is that these cooks have a mature level of patience needed to work with dough that requires a deft hand and a willingness to wait through multiple proofing processes, whether the final result is loaf, free-form, or single-serve.

179

KEY: **GF** Gluten Free   **VG** Vegan   **V** Vegetarian

Leah Newton
Dardanelle, Arkansas

Loaf by loaf, 17-year-old Leah Newton pays her way through college, baking the breads and rolls that have made her famous in her hometown of Russellville, Arkansas. Home-schooled her entire life, Leah also learned to cook and to garden the family's two large vegetable plots under her parents' tutelage. By the time she was grade school age, Leah was trying her hand at yeast-risen breads and found she had a natural proclivity for baking.

At 15 years old, she started selling her creations to friends and family, which led her to set up shop at her own table in the local farmers' market in 2011. Her business, One Nerd Bakery, paid for her first year at Arkansas Tech University, after which she will go to the French Pastry School in Chicago. The most important thing about making bread, Leah says, is the way it has tied her to her community, including selling bread at cost to the Crossing, a local coffeehouse that gives a portion of proceeds to local charities, and baking rolls for the Russ Bus, a local nonprofit, to distribute to the town's homeless.

Mediterranean Bread is Leah's signature recipe. It came about one day while she was trying to find a use for the leftover buttermilk and pesto in the family refrigerator.

"When it was in the oven the whole house smelled like a pizzeria, which was pretty cool because my parents met when they worked together at a pizzeria," says Leah. It was no surprise, then, that Mediterranean bread would be a Newton family favorite. But Leah was amazed when it became her biggest seller at the farmers' market. Local love of the bread prompted one customer to create "The Nerdy Club," an Italian meats and cheese sandwich made with Leah's bread. Other superfans make sure that Leah is always in the green by providing plenty of home-grown basil for the pesto—in trade for a couple of loaves, of course.

(continued)

MEDITERRANEAN BREAD

MAKES 3 SMALL LOAVES

1½ tablespoons active dry yeast

3 cups lukewarm water (110° to 115°F)

6½ cups all-purpose flour, plus more as needed

¼ cup buttermilk powder

1½ tablespoons coarse salt

1 cup pesto, store-bought or homemade (page 75 or 77)

⅓ cup chopped sun-dried tomatoes

Olive oil, for brushing the loaves

1. In a large bowl, dissolve the yeast in the warm water. In a separate bowl, combine the flour, buttermilk powder, and salt. Add the flour mixture to the yeast mixture. Mix well with a wooden spoon, cover loosely with plastic wrap, and set aside to rise for 2 hours.

2. In a bowl, stir together the pesto and sun-dried tomatoes. Set aside.

3. After the dough has risen, sprinkle the top with additional flour and divide the dough into thirds. Place one-third of the dough on a floured surface and, using a rolling pin, roll it out into a rectangle about 13 × 7 inches and ½ inch thick. Spread one-third of the pesto mixture over the dough rectangle and then roll the dough from the short end forward like a jelly roll and seal the edges. Set the log on a parchment-lined baking sheet seam side down. Repeat this step with the remaining dough balls and pesto mixture.

4. Allow the loaves to rise again in a warm, draft-free place for 20 minutes.

5. Meanwhile, preheat oven to 425°F during this second rise.

6. Once the dough has risen a second time, sprinkle each loaf with flour and, using a serrated knife, make three evenly spaced slashes across the top of each. Bake until golden brown, 30 to 40 minutes, brushing with olive oil halfway through the baking. Slice and serve.

Hannah Yee
San Francisco, California

Unlike her twin sister Megan (page 72), Hannah Yee is a more methodical cook who carefully plans what she'll be making for the once-a-month Kids Cook Dinner event that she and her sister have been doing for some years now. "My mom makes us plan and cook a whole meal for our family," says Hannah. "I like to plan and make parts of the meal all week, while my sister likes to plan and cook a whole meal in one day." One mealtime favorite is pizza made from dough that contains a good-amount of cornmeal for extra crispness. Since tomato sauce isn't popular in the Yee household, the pizzas take nontraditional forms, as in these **Cornmeal Pizza Dough Parmesan Crisps** that are great on their own or as crackers with cheese or meats. They may be stored in a zip-top bag for 3 days.

CORNMEAL PIZZA DOUGH PARMESAN CRISPS

MAKES ABOUT 12 CRISPS

Dough

- 1 teaspoon sugar
- 1 cup warm water (110° to 115°F)
- 1 envelope active dry yeast
- 1 cup cornmeal
- 2¼ cups all-purpose flour
- ¼ cup plus 1 teaspoon olive oil

Flavorings

- ½ cup pesto, store-bought or homemade (page 75 or 77)
- ½ cup grated Parmesan cheese
  Freshly ground black pepper

1. For the dough: Dissolve the sugar in the warm water and add the yeast. Stir gently until the yeast is dissolved. Allow the yeast to stand for about 5 minutes or until it starts to become frothy and bubbly.

2. In a large bowl, combine the cornmeal and flour. Measure out and set aside ¼ cup of the mixture to add later if needed.

3. Make a well in the middle of the flour mixture in the bowl and pour in ¼ cup of the oil and the yeast mixture. Using a wooden spoon, mix the flour into the well until the mixture forms a soft dough. Turn the dough out onto a lightly floured surface, dust your hands with flour, and knead the dough. Knead for 10 to 15 minutes, turning the dough 90 degrees every 5 minutes and continuing to need. Knead until the dough is smooth and springy and bounces back when touched. Add more of the flour/cornmeal mixture if the dough is too sticky. (Alternatively, in a stand mixer fitted with the dough hook, mix the cornmeal, flour, ¼ cup olive oil, and yeast mixture and knead for 5 minutes or until the dough springs back when touched.)

4. Add the remaining 1 teaspoon olive oil to a clean bowl and add the kneaded dough. Turn it once or twice so its entire surface is oiled. Cover the bowl with a kitchen towel and put in a warm, draft-free place to rise for 45 minutes.

5. Meanwhile, preheat the oven to 350°F. Line a baking sheet with parchment paper.

6. Punch down the dough and turn it out onto a floured surface. Using your hands, stretch the dough into a rectangle then use a rolling pin to roll it out to a 9 × 12-inch rectangle. Transfer the dough to the baking sheet. Brush the dough surface evenly with pesto and sprinkle with the Parmesan.

7. Bake the crisp on a baking sheet until it is lightly golden brown all over, 20 to 25 minutes. Remove and allow to cool. When the crisp is cool enough to handle use a bread knife to cut it into 2 × 3-inch pieces, like a large cracker. Serve with cheese or with soup.

Nathan Bailey
Reading, England, United Kingdom

Gluten-free since he was 11, 15-year-old Nathan Bailey acts as sous-chef for his mother, Christine, a nutritionist and UK cooking personality, when she makes television appearances and attends shows and events. A successful cook in his own right, the teen won his first cooking competition for kid-chefs in 2011 and has been a judge for the UK's FreeFrom Food Awards, tasting allergen-free products in order to make recommendations to other teens in Britain.

To Nathan, adopting a gluten-free lifestyle presented the challenge of adapting the recipes he was accustomed to cooking at his mom's side, but it was one he met admirably, starting a gluten-free cooking blog where he shares recipes and ideas. "I also help out in cookery demonstrations my mum runs for those with celiac disease and those wanting to learn about healthy gluten-free foods," he says. "I want to make gluten-free foods accessible to everyone and to highlight the problems faced by people wishing to eat healthfully and gluten-free." Nathan hopes to one day write a gluten-free cookbook for teenagers.

Nathan created **Gluten-Free Sun-Dried Tomato Muffins** as a lunch alternative to ever-popular sandwiches, and he suggests that it is versatile enough to spice up with a little chile pepper. "Sometimes I add olives to the mixture or fresh chopped herbs—rosemary is excellent," he says.

GLUTEN-FREE SUN-DRIED TOMATO MUFFINS

MAKES 1 DOZEN

1 cup gluten-free all-purpose baking flour

2 teaspoons gluten-free baking powder

½ teaspoon xanthan gum

⅛ teaspoon salt

⅛ teaspoon smoked paprika

½ cup shredded cheddar cheese

6 to 8 sun-dried tomatoes, finely chopped

6 tablespoons butter, melted and cooled

¾ cup milk

2 eggs

1. Preheat the oven to 350°F. Line the 12 cups of a muffin tin with paper liners.

2. In a medium bowl, mix together the all-purpose baking flour, baking powder, xanthan gum, salt, and paprika and stir thoroughly. Add the cheddar and sun-dried tomatoes and mix well.

3. In a large bowl, stir together the melted butter and milk. Beat in the eggs and mix until well combined.

4. Pour the flour mixture into the egg mixture and mix well. Spoon the batter into the muffin cups, filling each about halfway.

5. Bake until well risen and golden brown, 20 to 25 minutes. Let cool on a wire rack.

Alex Woodworth
Meriden, Connecticut

At age 14, Alex Woodworth faced a hard decision: legal punishment for a variety of petty crimes he'd committed after falling in with "the wrong crowd," or come to Chef Kashia Cave's program at My City Kitchen, a Meriden nonprofit that teaches healthy eating habits and fosters a sense of positive belonging among at-risk kids.

"I wasn't sure I was going to like it," says Alex. "But that first day we made an Asian stir-fry and I felt like it was the best thing I'd ever had. I sometimes think I'll never have anything as good as that dish I had that night."

He came back the next day and the day after, and today he has gone from being a "problem kid" to a superior student who has found through working with recipes that he loves math. The precision of baking also appeals to the young cook's sense of logic and order. "It's a science that requires focus and concentration so you don't mess up," says Alex.

In the 2 years that Alex has been with My City Kitchen, he's rapidly developed his skills to a near-professional level, appearing on television and at public demonstrations with Chef Kashia. In fact, Cave says, Alex Woodworth has basically become her go-to sous-chef.

While culinary school is always an option, he says he isn't quite sure what his future will bring. "I don't know what I'll be doing 20 years from now, but I do know I'll be eating and one thing is for sure—I'll be making something good."

Alex's **Asiago-Bacon Bread Pudding** is a sophisticated variation of a favorite Christmas morning dish made by his grandmother. While the original version is more like a bread casserole and used white bread, Alex's egg-bread version features a uniform texture that is ideal for slicing and pairs nicely with fresh fruit for breakfast or with a green salad for brunch or lunch.

ASIAGO-BACON BREAD PUDDING

MAKES 1 LOAF

6 slices hickory-smoked bacon or 2 pork sausage patties

10 slices brioche or other egg bread such as challah, crusts trimmed, and cut into 1-inch squares

2½ cups milk

6 eggs

½ teaspoon salt

¼ teaspoon freshly ground black pepper

1 teaspoon mustard powder

½ pound Asiago cheese, shredded

1. Preheat the oven to 350°F.

2. Heat a large skillet over medium-high heat and add the bacon or sausage. Cook until the bacon is crisp, about 5 minutes; or cook the sausage until well browned, 8 to 10 minutes. Remove from the pan with a slotted spoon and set aside.

3. In a large bowl, combine the bread and 1¼ cups of the milk and mix well.

4. In medium bowl, beat together the remaining 1¼ cups milk, the eggs, salt, pepper, and dry mustard. Pour this mixture over the bread mixture and mix very well.

5. Butter a 4 × 12-inch terrine or a deep 9-inch loaf pan. Spread one-quarter of the bread mixture onto the bottom of the pan and then sprinkle one-third of the Asiago on top. Layer one-third of the bacon or sausage on top of the cheese. Repeat with two more layers of bread, cheese, and bacon/sausage. End with a final layer of bread on top.

6. Place the pan in a large baking dish that can accommodate it easily. Pour enough water into the baking dish to reach about halfway up the sides of the loaf pan or terrine. Loosely cover the loaf or terrine pan with tin foil.

7. Bake the pudding until the mixture is puffy and set, about 40 minutes. Remove the foil and allow the top of the mixture to lightly brown.

8. Remove from the oven and cool for 15 minutes in the pan. Place a platter over the pan and turn it over. The pudding should release smoothly as one loaf. Cut into slices to serve.

Alyssa Pepin
Concord, New Hampshire

Alyssa Pepin remembers being a toddler, standing on a kitchen chair using a white spoon to mix up a batch of zucchini bread in a big brown bowl. The ingredients were simple she says, except for the most important one: love. Today, 16-year-old Alyssa is a student in the advanced culinary program at her high school in Concord, New Hampshire, but, she says, despite her more complex skills, love is the one ingredient she never cooks without.

"It's about how food can make a person feel," says the teen who most enjoys cooking with her friend Nick, who has Down syndrome, and is looking forward to her Girl Scout Gold Badge project teaching special needs' youngsters to cook healthy foods.

Alyssa hopes one day to go to culinary college and eventually on to France where, she believes, she can best perfect her baking skills. But, she says, no matter how advanced her skills become she still plans to make her family's **Zuchi Bread,** in the same brown bowl and using the same white spoon. "Of course," she says. "I don't need to stand on a kitchen chair any more!" This straightforward quick-bread recipe can be made healthier by substituting 2 cups of the all-purpose flour with white whole wheat flour. Zuchi Bread can be frozen after baking, in a zip-top bag, for up to 1 month.

ZUCHI BREAD

MAKES 1 LOAF

3 eggs
1 cup vegetable oil
1 tablespoon vanilla extract
2 cups grated zucchini
3 cups all-purpose flour
2 cups sugar
1 tablespoon ground cinnamon
1 teaspoon salt
1 teaspoon baking powder
½ teaspoon baking soda

1. Preheat the oven to 350°F. Grease an 8 × 4-inch loaf pan.

2. In a medium bowl, beat together the eggs, oil, and vanilla. Add the zucchini and mix well.

3. In another bowl, whisk together the flour, sugar, cinnamon, salt, baking powder, and baking soda. Add the flour mixture to the egg mixture and mix well so that it is thoroughly combined and forms a thick batter.

4. Pour the batter into the prepared loaf pan and bake until the top is golden brown and a cake tester comes out clean, 30 to 40 minutes.

Koa Halpern
Denver, Colorado

Fast food is not in 15-year-old Koa Halpern's vocabulary, nor on his menu. A vegetarian from an environmentally concerned family, it was not until his family hosted an exchange student from Korea that he began to consider bringing his personal mantra to the masses.

"The first thing she wanted to try when she arrived was American fast food—and she loved it," he says. "I was so intrigued by this that I wanted to understand why."

In trying to understand the crave-worthiness of fast food, Koa began to research the ingredient lists in some popular items and, he says, he was disturbed by what he found.

"I started doing experiments," says Koa. "I wanted to understand what the preservatives in fast food really did, so I made organic French fries and compared them with French fries from a well-known fast-food chain. The organic fries wilted in a few days and soon became covered in mold, but the fast-food fries looked as good as ever."

Koa left the fries on the plate for more than 3 years, observing how they were largely unchanged over time. "That experience taught me how processed fast food is. Not even mold will grow there," says the Colorado native whose experience inspired him to start Fast Food Free, a nonprofit that teaches people what exactly is in fast food, and encourages them—particularly kids—to take a pledge not to eat it.

The goal, he says, is not just to fight childhood obesity or heart disease or even cancer—but all of those things together. To date, thousands have taken the online pledge and Koa has been honored by *Parenting* magazine as a Kid Who Makes a Difference and identified by school-lunch evangelist Chef Ann Cooper as a Lunch Box Hero.

Koa only uses organic ingredients for his **Rosemary Bread**, a loaf that packs an herbaceous punch because of the quantity of rosemary he likes to use, but which nicely enhances its **Balsamic Dipping Sauce**. If you are not a fan of rosemary, feel free to reduce the amount by half. Thyme is a lighter herb with enough flavor to substitute for the rosemary as well.

(continued)

ROSEMARY BREAD WITH BALSAMIC DIPPING SAUCE

MAKES 2 LOAVES

1 teaspoon sugar

1 cup warm water (110° to 115°F)

1 envelope active dry yeast

3 cups unbleached white flour, plus more for dusting, as needed

½ cup whole wheat flour

2 tablespoons dried rosemary

Additional warm water, as needed

Olive oil, as needed

Balsamic Dipping Sauce (recipe follows)

1. Preheat the oven to 350°F. Dissolve the sugar in the warm water and add the yeast. Stir gently until the yeast is dissolved. Allow the yeast to stand for about 5 minutes or until it starts to become frothy and bubbly.

2. In a medium bowl, whisk together the white flour, whole wheat flour, and rosemary. Mix thoroughly.

3. When the yeast has dissolved, slowly pour the yeast mixture into the flour mixture, stirring with a wooden spoon. Add more water if needed, ¼ cup at a time, and continue stirring until the mixture forms a firm dough ball about the size of a grapefruit. If the dough is sticking to the side of the bowl you may need to add a bit more flour, 1 teaspoon at a time.

4. Cover the bowl with a damp cloth and set it in a warm, draft-free area to rise until doubled in size, about 1 hour.

5. Lightly punch down the dough and knead lightly for 5 to 7 minutes by hand or 3 to 5 minutes in a stand mixer using a dough hook on the low setting. The dough will be firm and smooth. Return the dough ball to the bowl and place a damp cloth over the bowl. Allow it to rise a second time for about 30 minutes.

6. Preheat the oven to 375°F. Line a baking sheet with parchment paper.

7. After the dough has risen a second time, turn the dough out onto a lightly floured board and divide in half using a large knife. Roll out each half into a cylinder about 1 foot in length and 1½ to 2 inches in diameter. Place the loaves on the baking sheet.

8. Score the top of the loaves diagonally with a sharp knife at about 2-inch intervals. Lightly brush the top of each loaf with olive oil. Bake for about 45 minutes. When done, the surface will be lightly browned and the loaves will sound hollow when thumped on the bottom.

9. Serve the bread with balsamic dipping sauce on the side.

Balsamic Dipping Sauce

Koa Halpern's dipping sauce for his Rosemary Bread works well with Mediterranean Bread (page 182) too. Alternatively, it works incredibly well as a salad dressing!

¼ cup extra virgin olive oil
2 tablespoons balsamic vinegar
¼ teaspoon dried oregano
1 clove garlic, minced
⅛ teaspoon freshly ground black pepper
⅛ teaspoon salt

In a screwtop jar, combine all ingredients and set aside for at least 1 hour before using. Shake well once more just before serving.

Zachary Reiser
Westport, Connecticut

One of Zachary Reiser's earliest forays into cooking was roasting clams with his grandfather in the backyard of his Westport, Connecticut, home. Food preparation, he says, has always been a way to connect in his family. "My family likes to discuss the recipe and what could have been changed or done differently as much as we enjoy actually eating the food," he says.

Joining the advanced culinary team at his high school taught him that food is also a way to connect with others. Last fall, Zachary and other student chefs from the program were featured guests at the local farmers' market. In order to do the best job, the group came together like a family, he says. "We ordered ourselves professional chef wear, embroidered with our names and on the day of the farmers' market, we arrived and set up, with four tables huddled under our small tent to keep out of the slight drizzle that was coming down."

Working as a team, the group perused the different vendors' stalls to see what was fresh that day, in order to decide what to cook for sale. They settled on strawberry/apple compote with goat cheese and thyme on a baguette and a baby yellow tomato-spinach sauté, also on a baguette.

Zachary's **Chocolate Chip Pumpkin Bread** is an adaptation of a recipe given to his mother by a family friend some years ago. He's changed the recipe to use fresh roasted pumpkin and more chocolate to satisfy his sweet tooth.

CHOCOLATE CHIP PUMPKIN BREAD

MAKES 2 LOAVES

- 3 cups all-purpose flour
- 2 teaspoons baking powder
- 2 teaspoons baking soda
- 1¼ teaspoons ground cinnamon
- 1 teaspoon salt
- ¾ teaspoon ground cloves
- ½ teaspoon ground ginger
- ¼ teaspoon ground mace
- 2 cups dark brown sugar
- 1½ cups vegetable oil
- 4 eggs, beaten
- 2 cups pumpkin puree, canned or homemade (recipe follows)
- 8 ounces chocolate chips

1. Preheat the oven to 350°F. Grease two 8 × 4-inch loaf pans.

2. In a medium bowl, sift together the flour, baking powder, baking soda, cinnamon, salt, cloves, ginger, and mace.

3. In another large bowl, beat together the brown sugar and oil. Stir in the eggs and pumpkin puree and beat until thoroughly combined.

4. Mix the dry ingredients into the pumpkin mixture until the flour is fully incorporated.

Do not overmix. Add the chocolate chips and stir until just combined.

5. Pour the batter into the prepared pans and bake until a cake tester comes out clean, about 55 minutes.

6. Cool in the pans for 15 to 20 minutes, then remove the loaves from the pans. May be frozen in zip-top bags for up to 1 month.

Pumpkin Puree

MAKES 3 TO 4 CUPS

A number of recipes in this book call for pumpkin puree, which you can buy canned or make yourself for fresher flavor.

   1 large pie pumpkin
     Cooking spray

1. Preheat the oven to 400°F. Light coat a baking sheet with cooking spray.

2. Slice the stem end off and halve the pumpkin lengthwise. Scrape out the seeds and stringy fibers using a spoon. Cut each half in half again and place the pumpkin pieces on the baking sheet. Roast the pumpkin quarters until they are fork-tender, about 45 minutes.

3. Allow the cooked pumpkin pieces to cool until they can be comfortably handled.

Using a knife, scrape the flesh away from the skin and into a food processor. Process until smooth.

4. Place the pumpkin puree in a fine mesh sieve suspended over a large bowl and allow the liquid to drip out. Remove enough excess liquid so the pumpkin is the consistency of a thick spread, rather than a thick liquid.

5. Store in an airtight container in the refrigerator for up to 2 weeks.

Brooks Lange
Reno, Nevada

Thirteen-year-old Brooks Lange is the son of popular food blogger Lori Lange, better known as *Recipe Girl*. Always in the kitchen, spatula at the ready, Brooks worked alongside his mom as her sous-chef for the website, at cooking demonstrations, and as part of a spokes duo for McCormick spices.

By the time he was 10, however, the young cook was ready to branch out on his own and persuaded his parents to let him start his own website, *RecipeBoy—Growing Up Foodie*. Because Brooks really likes math, he prefers baking because of the precise measurements required for success, although he will cook just about everything and is looking forward to a long-term culinary career.

"I want to cook consistently as I grow up. I feel like it will help me in the future," he says. "Plus, my dad says that the chicks dig a guy who can cook."

Brooks's **Raspberry Dark Chocolate Banana Bread** gets an additional flavor pop through his addition of tart raspberries and bittersweet chocolate. Unlike traditional quick-bread recipes that feature a lot of butter and oil, Brooks's version makes use of low-fat yogurt to achieve a moist and less-fatty loaf.

RASPBERRY DARK CHOCOLATE
BANANA BREAD

Cooking spray

2 cups all-purpose flour

¾ teaspoon baking soda

½ teaspoon salt

1 cup sugar

4 tablespoons (½ stick) unsalted butter, at room temperature

2 large eggs

1½ cups mashed ripe banana (about 3 bananas)

⅓ cup low-fat plain yogurt

1 teaspoon vanilla extract

1 cup dark chocolate chunks or chips

1 cup raspberries, tossed in 1 tablespoon all-purpose flour

Additional raspberries and chocolate chunks, for garnish (optional)

1. Preheat the oven to 350°F. Coat a 9 × 5-inch loaf pan with cooking spray.

2. In a medium bowl, whisk together the flour, baking soda, and salt.

3. In a separate large bowl, with an electric mixer, beat the sugar and butter at medium speed until well blended, about 1 minute. Add the eggs one at a time, beating well after each addition. Add the banana, yogurt, and vanilla and beat until blended. Beat in the flour mixture and mix until just combined. Don't overmix. Stir in the chocolate chunks and then gently fold in the raspberries, reserving some of each for the top of the bread.

4. Spoon the batter into the prepared pan and bake until a cake tester comes out clean, 50 to 60 minutes. Halfway through baking, sprinkle the bread with the reserved chocolate and raspberries.

5. When the bread is finished, remove and cool 15 minutes in the pan on a wire rack. Turn out of the pan onto the rack to cool completely.

Erica Barry
McLean, Virginia

Erica Barry was first bitten by the cooking bug when, at age 10, she threw together a quick grilled cheese sandwich to which she added ham and pear slices. "I posted it on Allrecipes and I felt like the next Bobby Flay," says the now-16-year-old. "I was amazed how much great feedback I got for this seemingly trivial little sandwich, and the thought of other people actually making my recipe and enjoying it was so exciting that I've been experimenting in the kitchen ever since."

Soon after, Erica started the blog *Cannella Vita,* which is Italian for "Cinnamon Life," as a way to share her recipes with a wider audience. The blog is so named because of the teen's passion for cinnamon, which she touts for both its taste and its health benefits. The blog, she says, has more than satisfied the craving for feedback that she first got with that original grilled cheese posting.

"I'm greatly influenced by all those amazing people out there who take the time to write to me about recipes, ask questions, and tell me how it turned out and how they enjoyed it. The way I see it, they are putting time and effort into trying out one of my recipes and putting the dish on their dinner tables for their families," says the teen who is also an avid runner and yogini. "There is an element of trust and responsibility there that is rare for a young person to experience, and it is such an honor that they put their trust in me. That faith has made me test and re-test recipes, making sure that they are the best that they can be."

Erica's **Cannella Vita Cinnamon Buns** recipe is easily her signature dish, but it does require some physical stamina to make the croissant dough. "But hang in there," Erica says. "It's a great arm workout! And the end results—a flaky, delicate croissant-like bun—are well worth it."

(continued)

The Versatility of Croissant Dough

Croissant dough, like that in Erica Barry's cinnamon bun recipe, is a "laminate" dough, so called because multiple layers of dough surround and laminate multiple layers of butter. Puff pastry, when made properly, is another laminate dough that most cooks are familiar with. There is no doubt that croissant dough is labor-intensive and that's why only a few bakeries make this their specialty; however, once made, croissant dough is incredibly versatile for use not just as traditional croissants but as stuffed pastries for both sweet and savory fillings. You may freeze finished croissant dough completely instead of chilling it as a last step, for use later. If you choose to do this, be sure to allow the dough to defrost in the refrigerator before rolling it out for use in your final preparation.

CANNELLA VITA
CINNAMON BUNS

Croissant dough

- 4 cups all-purpose flour, plus more for rolling out the dough
- ¼ cup plus 2 tablespoons sugar
- 1 tablespoon plus 1 scant teaspoon instant yeast
- 2¼ teaspoons salt
- ½ cup plus 2 tablespoons lukewarm water
- ½ cup plus 2 tablespoons milk heated to 110° to 115°F
- 3 tablespoons unsalted butter, at room temperature
- 8 ounces (2 sticks) cold unsalted butter

Cinnamon filling

- ½ cup brown sugar
- ½ cup granulated sugar
  Finely grated zest of 2 medium oranges
- 2 tablespoons ground cinnamon
- ⅛ teaspoon salt

1. For the croissant dough: In a stand mixer fitted with a dough hook, whisk together the flour, sugar, yeast, and salt. Add the water, milk, and room-temperature butter. Mix on low speed for 3 minutes, then at medium speed for an additional 3 minutes, until it is smooth and elastic.

2. Flour the dough lightly then wrap it well in plastic and refrigerate overnight.

3. Cut the cold butter lengthwise into 3 equal slabs per stick and arrange the pieces on a sheet of parchment paper to form a 6-inch square. Top the butter square with another sheet of parchment and pound the butter with even strokes using a rolling pin. As the pieces begin to stick together, press down with the rolling pin and roll it into a 7½-inch square.

4. Using a sharp paring knife, trim the edges of the butter to make a sharp square. Add the trimmings to the center of the square and continue pounding and smoothing the square. Do not let the butter square become larger than 7½ inches. Refrigerate the butter while you roll out the dough.

5. Remove the dough from the refrigerator and unwrap it on a lightly floured surface. Roll it into a 10½-inch square.

6. Take the butter square out of the refrigerator, unwrap, and place it on the dough so that butter square is centered in the dough square. Fold two sides of dough inward over the butter so that they meet in the middle like an envelope. You will have to pull the dough a bit to make it meet and then press down on the seam. Press the edges together to completely seal the butter inside the dough.

7. Lightly flour the top and bottom of the dough and roll it out into an 8 × 24-inch rectangle, focusing on lengthening rather than widening. Pick up the bottom short end of the dough and fold it a third of the way over the dough, and then fold the dough again so that the dough is folded the way you would fold a business letter. Wrap a piece of parchment loosely around this folded dough and freeze for 20 minutes.

8. Repeat step 7, rolling and folding the dough, two more times. It's important to freeze the dough each time. Then cover the dough and refrigerate overnight.

9. Unwrap and lightly flour the top and bottom of the dough. Roll the dough into a 12 × 20-inch rectangle. Using a spray bottle, mist the dough lightly with water.

10. For the cinnamon filling: In a small bowl, mix together the sugars, orange zest, cinnamon, and salt.

11. Sprinkle the cinnamon mixture over the dough. Starting at a long side, roll the dough up as you would a jelly roll. Using a sharp knife, slice the roll crosswise into 12 cinnamon buns and place each bun, cut side up, inside the cup of a well-greased muffin pan. Refrigerate overnight.

12. The next morning, take the rolls out of the fridge and let rest at room temperature for 1 hour.

13. Preheat the oven to 375°F.

14. Bake until the buns are dark golden brown, 20 to 25 minutes. Remove from the pan immediately. Serve warm or at room temperature.

CHAPTER 7

Sweet!

(Desserts/Confections)

O ne of the most storied marriages of science and art in the kitchen can be found in the preparation of desserts. In this chapter our young chefs turn their hands to making the final and most beloved course of any meal. Here you'll find confections spun not just from sugar, but also from more unique sweeteners such as dates, maple syrup, mashed fruit, and condensed milk. As in the rest of the book, these recipes feature a wide variety of ethnic flavors and techniques, many of them original and based on the experimentation of the individual cook. Perhaps most interesting is the variety of purpose-built recipes for those with food intolerances and allergies, and the cooks' heavy reliance on natural flavors from fruit and nuts rather than artificial flavorings, syrups, or candies.

KEY: **GF** Gluten Free   **VG** Vegan   **V** Vegetarian

Taylor Miller
St. Petersburg, Florida

A diagnosis of celiac disease when he was 14 pushed Taylor Miller into the kitchen. "I learned that being gluten-free meant taking a lot of foods out of my diet," says Taylor, who is now 16. "Most people who were gluten free seemed to be upset with what they ate and made it seem like a terrible thing. So I set out to change that for myself, and then I realized I could help people out along the way by sharing what I came up with."

The result is the blog *Gluten Away*, where the Florida teen shares recipes that he develops as well as tips for gluten-free eating during the holidays and when dining out. Taylor has also been delving into making foods that are safe for other allergy sufferers. If you like commercial peanut butter cup candies, then these **Gluten-Free Peanut Butter–Chocolate Candy Bars** will earn a permanent place in your heart. Created for a more sophisticated palate that appreciates darker chocolate, the bars are less sweet than mainstream varieties. Because being food inclusive is a hallmark of Taylor's cuisine, he's developed alternative ingredients for making these candies so they may also be made dairy free and peanut free.

GLUTEN-FREE PEANUT BUTTER–CHOCOLATE CANDY BARS

MAKES 4 DOZEN SMALL BARS

- 1 stick butter or ½ cup Earth Balance Natural Butter for dairy free
- 2 cups natural peanut butter or soy, almond or sunflower seed butter for peanut-free
- 1 teaspoon gluten-free vanilla extract
- ½ cup packed brown sugar
- 2 cups powdered sugar, sifted
- 2 cups semisweet chocolate chips

1. Melt the butter or margarine over low heat in a medium saucepan. Stir in the peanut butter and vanilla and mix well with a wooden spoon.

2. Add the brown sugar and stir well over low heat until completely combined. Remove the pan from the heat, add the powdered sugar, and mix well until totally combined. The mixture will look like thick cookie batter.

3. Press the mixture evenly into a 9 x 13-inch baking dish or, ideally, a jelly roll pan that has been lightly sprayed with baking spray. Refrigerate the pan for 1 hour.

4. Pour the chocolate chips into a medium microwave-safe bowl and microwave on high for 1 minute. Stir the chocolate with a rubber spatula, and continue to microwave on high for 1 minute intervals or until the chocolate is totally melted, 3 minutes at the most.

5. Remove the pan from the refrigerator and pour the melted chocolate over the peanut-butter mixture. Spread with a small or rubber off-set spatula. Shake the baking dish gently to ensure that the chocolate is distributed evenly. Chill in the refrigerator until the bars are completely set, about 1 hour. Slice into 48 2 x 2-inch squares. The bars can be stored in an airtight container in layers separated by wax paper for up to one week.

Sophia Hunt
Brooklyn, New York

Culture crossing is food blogger Sophia Hunt's main inspiration when it comes to cooking. Of both Brazilian and fifth generation Scottish-Welsh-English descent, Sophia is also an avid singer involved in several choirs. "My culinary style is a combination of everything that makes me who I am," says the 16-year-old. "My two cultures bring in a combination of flavors that are not only comforting, like pecan pie, but tropical and fresh, like a shrimp stew made with coconut milk. And all of the time I spend on music brings in a creative aspect that always keeps me creative."

Right now, she is working on a food-based community outreach program in her mom's native Brazil.

"My aunt has a small farm near the outskirts of the city she is from, and the farm is in a very poor town. Our plan is to spend a week at the village school, teaching kids some simple American dishes they can easily replicate at home with the ingredients they have available, like chocolate chip cookies and brownies," she says. "This will give them a tool, because not only can they make these and sell them to earn a little extra money, but they also learn basic cooking and baking skills to pursue jobs in the culinary industry."

On her blog, *Sophia's Sweets*, the Brooklynite shares her passion for baked goods, and she says she hopes to open her own bakery one day, or even create her own cooking show that she plans to name "The Singing Chef."

Her **Giandujia Raspberry Sandwich Cookies** were inspired by *brigadeiro,* a chewy chocolate truffle made in Brazil. The chocolate flavor is intense enough to be a complement to a cup of good strong coffee or even espresso.

GIANDUJIA RASPBERRY SANDWICH COOKIES

MAKES ABOUT 1 DOZEN

- 3 egg whites, at room temperature
- 1½ cups powdered sugar, divided, plus additional for dusting
- ½ cup unsweetened cocoa powder
- 2 tablespoons cornstarch
- ½ teaspoon salt
- 1 (13-ounce) jar hazelnut chocolate spread such as Nutella
- ½ cup chopped bittersweet chocolate or bittersweet chocolate chips
- ⅓ cup hot chocolate mix or cocoa powder sweetened with 1 tablespoon of sugar, for rolling cookies
- ⅓ cup raspberry jam or jelly

1. Preheat the oven to 350°F. Line two baking sheets with parchment paper.

2. With a stand mixer, or using an electric hand mixer on high speed, beat the egg whites until they hold soft peaks, about 2 to 3 minutes. Gradually add ½ cup of the powdered sugar, until the mixture has doubled in volume and has the consistency of marshmallow spread, about 3 minutes.

3. In a medium bowl, sift together the remaining 1 cup powdered sugar, unsweetened cocoa powder, cornstarch, and salt. Add the cocoa mixture to the egg mixture on low speed, until just incorporated. Quickly and lightly fold in the chocolate spread and chopped bittersweet chocolate. Refrigerate dough for 30 minutes.

4. Using a tablespoon or 1-ounce ice cream scoop, scoop the dough into small balls. Roll these balls in the sweetened cocoa powder and arrange them at least 1-inch apart on the cookie sheets, to allow room for spreading.

5. Bake the cookies for 10 minutes. The edges should be firm to the touch, but the centers will be very soft. Remove the cookies from the oven and allow them to cool completely on the baking sheets.

6. Spread 1 to 2 teaspoons of raspberry jam on bottom side of one cookie and then sandwich another cookie onto it. Repeat until all the sandwiches have been made. Dust completed cookies with powdered sugar before serving.

Mikey Robins
Lower Gwynedd, Pennsylvania

A contestant on Food Network's teen edition of *Chopped,* 15-year-old Mikey Robins spent many of his formative years helping out at his parents' kids' cooking school in North Wales, Pennsylvania. "Once I had mastered all the classes, I began teaching and hosting birthday parties for our younger kids in the school," says Mikey, the youngest person to ever win a *Chopped* challenge.

Staging the perfect event is just as important as the food itself to Mikey, who is a performer in community theater. "I'm also a caterer and party planner," says the teen whose catering and party planning company, Events by Mikey, is now in its second year. "I don't just cook for my guests, I plan an evening they'll never forget from tablescapes to invitations, to floral displays, goodie bags, and much more."

Mikey Robins serves **Cranberry-Pumpkin Biscotti** with coffee or in goodie bags for his catering clients' guests. The double-baking process is what gives these biscuits their hard, crumbly texture.

CRANBERRY-PUMPKIN BISCOTTI

MAKES ABOUT 1 DOZEN

2½ cups all-purpose flour

1 cup granulated sugar

1 teaspoon baking powder

1 teaspoon ground cinnamon

1 teaspoon pumpkin pie spice

⅛ teaspoon salt

2 eggs

¾ cup pumpkin puree, canned or homemade (page 195)

1 teaspoon vanilla extract

⅓ cup dried cranberries

Powdered sugar, for dusting

1. Preheat the oven to 350°F. Line a baking sheet with parchment paper or coat with cooking spray.

2. In a medium bowl, stir together the flour, granulated sugar, baking powder, cinnamon, pumpkin pie spice, and salt.

3. In another bowl, gently whisk together the eggs, pumpkin puree, vanilla, and cranberries. Pour the pumpkin mixture into the flour mixture and stir to incorporate the ingredients, until the dough is crumbly.

4. Turn the dough out onto a floured surface and knead until it holds together without crumbling. Transfer the dough to the baking sheet and form into a large log about 15 inches long by 6 to 7 inches wide and $\frac{1}{2}$ inch high. Bake until the center is firm to the touch, 25 to 30 minutes. (Leave the oven on but reduce the temperature to 300°F.)

5. Let the loaf cool for 20 minutes and then, using a serrated knife, slice the log crosswise into 1-inch-wide slices. Return these slices to the baking sheet. Bake the biscotti until crisp but not browned, another 15 to 20 minutes.

6. Let the biscotti cool completely. Dust with powdered sugar. Biscotti may be stored in an airtight container for up to 1 week.

Sunnie Heers
Las Vegas, Nevada

Sunnie Heers describes her cooking style as "sneaky." "I love sneaking veggies into every single meal, whether it's adding big handful of greens to an omelet, a bit of avocado to a smoothie, or juicing a cucumber along with oranges for orange juice," says the high school junior from Las Vegas. "Veggies are like superheroes, fighting all the bad guys and bringing you good health." A proponent of raw and vegan cooking, Sunnie says she lets the ingredients do the work for her. "If I have good quality ingredients, I just have to find the ones that get along well and put them together," says the teen who recalls writing "new spices" above "Barbies" on her Christmas list when she was a little girl. "I also use real food in all my recipes, not only for health but because unprocessed ingredients make such a difference in taste," says Sunnie, who writes about her food adventures at the blog *Modern Girl Nutrition*.

Sunnie developed her **Almond Energy Squares** as a way, she says, to give her pocketbook a break from buying the raw food energy bars she likes so much. Experimenting with what was in her kitchen, she threw five simple ingredients together to produce a tiny toothsome snack with a pleasing texture. Small as they are, they are delightfully satisfying and a perfect go-to mid-afternoon nibble.

ALMOND ENERGY SQUARES

MAKES 8 SMALL SQUARES

½ cup almonds

5 dates, pitted and chopped

¼ teaspoon of salt

1 teaspoon cinnamon

1 heaping tablespoon almond nut butter

1. Place the almonds in a blender or food processor and blend until they are finely chopped.

2. Add the dates to the almond meal along with the salt and cinnamon. Pulse until well mixed.

3. Add the almond butter and pulse for 15 to 30 seconds or until the mixture sticks together and comes away from the sides of the bowl.

4. Using a rubber spatula, remove mixture from the blender or food processor and spread onto a cutting board that has been sprayed with cooking spray.

5. Using the rubber spatula, spread and push the mixture into a 1-inch-thick 4 x 8-inch rectangle. Cut into 1 x 2-inch rectangles. May be stored in a sealed container, separated by pieces of wax paper, for up to 3 days at room temperature, or refrigerated for 1 week.

Deanna Baris
Westport, Connecticut

When Deanna Baris was 8 years old, she was put on sweet-potato peeling duty for her family's Thanksgiving feast. Sixteen potatoes later, she was even more excited to get into the kitchen. Today, the 17-year-old shares her passion for sweets on her blog *DB and Jelly: Adventures in Teenage Baking,* which she started when she was 14. In looking for colleges, the teen says she's on the hunt for a campus where there is an opportunity for her to keep cooking. "I don't know how I'll survive without my kitchen!" she says. Deanna's **Breakfast Cookies** have become a family staple because not only are they grab-and-go, but they also balance sweetness with wholesome ingredients. "They're made with whole wheat flour, flaxseed, bananas, and peanut butter, so they're actually healthy!" she quips. "Honestly, any excuse to eat a cookie for breakfast is good with me."

BREAKFAST COOKIES

MAKES ABOUT 18 LARGE BREAKFAST COOKIES

¾ cup whole wheat pastry flour

¾ cup all-purpose flour

1 cup rolled oats

2 tablespoons flaxmeal

1 teaspoon baking powder

¼ teaspoon ground cinnamon

¼ teaspoon salt

1 egg

¼ cup tightly packed brown sugar

1 tablespoon vanilla extract

1 ripe banana, mashed

1½ tablespoons honey

4 tablespoons (½ stick) butter, at room temperature

2 tablespoons creamy peanut butter, melted

½ cup dark chocolate chips

1. Preheat the oven to 325°F. Line a baking sheet with parchment paper or coat with baking spray.

2. In a medium bowl, mix together the flours, oats, flaxmeal, baking powder, cinnamon, and salt. Set aside.

3. In a large bowl, whisk together the egg and brown sugar until smooth. Beat in the vanilla, mashed banana, honey, butter, and melted peanut butter and blend well.

4. Gradually add the flour mixture to the banana mixture, a little at a time, mixing gently until it just comes together. Add the chocolate chips and stir to distribute.

5. Spoon out the dough 2 tablespoons at a time and arrange on baking sheet 1 inch apart. Bake until the cookies are golden brown and a cake tester inserted comes out clean, 10 to 12 minutes. Cool on racks.

Allison Schwartz
Penn Valley, Pennsylvania

"I come from a long line of foodies," says 17-year-old Allison Schwartz. "One of my great-grandfathers owned and operated a pickle factory in the 1920s and another owned and operated a confections factory. My uncle currently owns a Jewish bakery on Long Island, and my grandmother and mother are simply exquisite cooks."

Even though the teen describes herself and her family as "basically food-obsessed," she says she didn't realize her passion fully until she got to high school and was able to take culinary classes that opened her eyes to more than cooking. She also learned about food policy issues, prompting her to campaign for nutrition labels and locally sourced food in the school cafeteria.

Allison also started a blog called *The Baking Year* in her junior year of high school. "Having the blog kept me connected to baking and allowed me to find time to bake amongst everything else that was going on," she says. "It inspired me to try new, daring recipes that I might not have otherwise."

Her specialty dish is her great-grandmother Lily's **Mandelbrot,** which she uses as a reliable base for different levels of experimentation. "I change the basic recipe each time I make it by using various add-ins," she says of the cookie that most closely resembles Italian biscotti. "These can range from chocolate chips, dried cherries, dried cranberries, dried apricots, to anything else."

MANDELBROT

1 cup vegetable oil

1 cup plus 2 tablespoons sugar

3 eggs

1 teaspoon vanilla extract

1 teaspoon almond extract

1 tablespoon grated orange zest

2 cups all-purpose flour

2 cups almond meal

1 teaspoon salt

1 teaspoon baking powder

2½ teaspoons ground cinnamon

1 cup sliced almonds

Optional add-ins, such as chocolate chips or dried fruit

1. Preheat the oven to 325°F. Line a baking sheet with parchment paper.

2. In a bowl, with an electric mixer, blend the oil and 1 cup of the sugar for about 2 minutes. Add the eggs, vanilla and almond extracts, and orange zest and blend thoroughly, about 1 minute.

3. In another bowl, combine the flour, almond meal, salt, baking powder, and 2 teaspoons of the cinnamon. Whisk well to combine.

4. Add the flour mixture to the oil mixture in three parts, mixing between each addition until just combined. Mix in the sliced almonds and any additions as desired. Stir until combined.

5. Divide the dough into 4 or 5 portions and shape each into an oval loaf on the baking sheet, with about 2 inches of space between them. Loaves should be about 2 inches wide and 1 inch high. Mix together the remaining 2 tablespoons sugar and ½ teaspoon cinnamon and sprinkle on the loaves.

6. Bake for 45 minutes. Remove the loaves from the oven and cut them crosswise into 1-inch-thick slices. Place the slices cut side down on the baking sheet and return them to the oven for another 5 to 10 minutes, depending on how crisp you like them. Transfer the mandelbrot to cooling racks to cool completely. Mandelbrot may be stored in an airtight container for up to 1 week.

The Entrepreneurs

Mia Alessi

Parkton, Maryland

Some young chefs cook for a cause and others simply for the love of being in the kitchen, while still others turn their skills to adult-level business propositions. Leah Newton turned her love for baking into a farmers' market business robust enough to help her pay her way through her first years of college (page 181). Kenny Seals-Nutt (page 41) and Mikey Robins (page 210) are both teen caterers scoring very adult jobs with their sophisticated foods. For Hanalei Edbrooke (page 130), food entrepreneurship is more of a microbusiness with which she funds other personal projects.

Mia Alessi takes her version of the food business a step further with a custom persona that she adopts when selling her homemade cake mixes. Known as "Bratty Crocker," Mia dresses in a Raggedy Ann-esque costume and makeup when appearing at local farmers' markets and other events to sell her MMM Mischief in a Mug Cake. Her stage name—a riff on the mythical cake-mix queen Betty Crocker—came about when, as early as age 5, Mia quickly proved she had her own way of doing things in the kitchen. Focus and determination may have made the youngster a bit . . . domineering.

"We started calling her Bratty Crocker," her mom Michele laughs. "It's all in good fun." Mia, who is now 12, also does in-costume cooking demonstrations around her town. Here is **Bratty Crocker's** take on a classic **Amish-Style Sugar Cookie,** which you will find has a more "cakey" texture than traditional sugar cookies.

Bratty Crocker's Amish-Style Sugar Cookies

MAKES 3 DOZEN

1 cup canola oil
2¼ cups sugar, plus more for sprinkling
3 eggs
2 teaspoons vanilla or almond extract
3½ cups all-purpose flour
1 tablespoon baking powder
1 teaspoon baking soda
1 teaspoon cream of tartar
1 teaspoon salt
1 cup sour cream

1. Preheat the oven to 350°F. Line 2 baking sheets with parchment or coat with baking spray.

2. In a large bowl, mix together the oil and sugar with a wooden spoon until totally combined. Beat in the eggs one at time until well mixed and smooth. Stir in the vanilla or almond extract.

3. In a separate bowl, whisk together the flour, baking powder, baking soda, cream of tartar, and salt.

4. Add the flour mixture to the oil mixture in thirds, alternating with the sour cream. Beat well so that the dough is completely mixed. The dough will be thick, smooth, and sticky, but not as stiff as traditional cookie dough.

5. Spoon the batter by tablespoons about 3 inches apart onto the baking sheets. Sprinkle each cookie with additional sugar.

6. Bake until the edges start to turn golden brown, 12 to 14 minutes. Let the cookies cool on a wire rack.

Chloe Jones
Pelham, New York

Avid teen baker Chloe Jones says her family went from food crazy to health-food crazy when her mom enrolled in school to become a nutritionist. "Because of her studying to be a nutritionist, my whole family sort of became nutritionists with her," says the 15-year-old who counts a recent family trip to France as one of the most memorable food experiences in her young life.

"I wasn't ever really an adventurous eater, but on that trip I tried everything, and I mean *everything*, and it was amazing," she says. "Foods I didn't like on their own could be something totally amazing and different when paired with something else. Suddenly the culinary world was my oyster and I couldn't open my mouth wide enough."

One of Chloe's favorite recipes is **Gluten-Free Chocolate Chip Cookies** that she adapted with her gluten-free dad in mind. "I created this recipe when my dad became gluten-free and I felt bad that he couldn't eat the baked goods I made," says Chloe. "This recipe also came about because my mom isn't fan of the processed gluten-free baked goods on the market. We were thrilled when we found out oats were gluten-free and could be processed into homemade oat flour."

DIY Gluten-Free Flours

Once upon a time, those suffering with gluten-related illnesses had to resign themselves to a life without bread or dessert. Now, there are a wide variety of gluten-free flours available even in mainstream grocery stores. Many of them can be made at home, including oat flour (as in Chloe's cookies here), as well as rice and chickpea flour, but an industrial strength blender or grinder is needed for rice and chickpea flour. For both, simply grind the whole grains of rice or dried chickpeas in a grinder or food processor that may specifically be used with grains. Grind into a fine powder and sift the resulting flour with a fine-mesh sieve to remove any unground parts of the kernels. Freshly ground rice or chickpea flours can be stored in a zip-top bag or airtight container for up to 2 months.

GLUTEN-FREE
CHOCOLATE CHIP COOKIES

MAKES 3 DOZEN

1½ cups gluten-free rolled oats

¼ cup almond flour

⅓ cup millet flour

1 teaspoon baking soda

½ teaspoon salt

8 tablespoons (1 stick) butter, melted

⅓ cup brown sugar

¼ cup granulated sugar

1 large egg

1 teaspoon vanilla extract

12 ounces gluten-free semisweet or bittersweet chocolate chips

2 tablespoons shredded unsweetened coconut (optional)

1. Preheat the oven to 375°F. Line 2 large baking sheets with parchment paper.

2. Place the oats in a food processor and pulse or grind until they reach the consistency of flour. In a large bowl, whisk together the oat flour, almond flour, and millet flour. Add the baking soda and salt and whisk well.

3. In a bowl, with an electric mixer, beat the melted butter and two sugars on low speed until they are a creamy consistency, 1 to 2 minutes in a stand mixer, 3 to 4 minutes with a handheld mixer.

4. Add the egg and vanilla and mix well to combine completely. Slowly add the flour mixture until it is just incorporated. Do not overmix. Next add in the chocolate chips and shredded coconut (if using).

5. Using a 1-tablespoon cookie scoop or a tablespoon, portion out balls of dough and place 2 inches apart on the baking sheets. The cookies will spread a lot when baked. (There is enough dough to make at least one more batch; be sure to let the baking sheets cool between batches.)

6. Bake until the cookies are puffy and lightly browned, 8 to 10 minutes, rotating the sheets back to front about halfway through baking. Let the cookies cool on the sheets on cooling racks.

Alessandra Peters
Aberdeen, Scotland, United Kingdom

"I'm a third-culture kid," says 15-year-old Alessandra Peters, also known as the Food Intolerant Teen. "I was born in Oman, moved to Syria, Holland, Qatar, and now Scotland, and I still have vivid memories of the fruit vendors lining the streets of Damascus on an early Saturday morning and sweet Qatari women grinding za'atar to sprinkle on their freshly baked Arabic bread."

Alessandra's love affair with food changed dramatically when she was diagnosed with celiac disease and many other food allergies when she was 12. "When I was diagnosed my life changed. A lot. For the better."

The teen, whose *Foodie Teen* website chronicles her adventures cooking vegan, Paleo, grain-free, dairy-free, and soy-free foods, counts herself lucky to be food intolerant—because of the world of possibility it has opened up for her cooking. "I make everything completely from scratch," she says. "So that means if a recipe uses chocolate, I'll go and make some chocolate using cacao butter, agave nectar, and ground cacao nibs."

Alessandra fuels her hunger for culinary knowledge by taking college-level nutrition and food science courses from online institutions worldwide, which, she says, makes her a better cook.

At the top of the teen's agenda is exploding the misconceptions that allergy-free food isn't as good as "regular food." "I thrive on whole, organic foods and strive to support other children in the same situation as myself," she says. "It is a lifetime goal of mine to show people that having allergies is not at all bad and that it is a great way to learn how to cook new, exciting, and, most importantly, delicious dishes."

Alessandra's **Chocolate Pecan Cookies** came about as a fluke while she was trying to make gluten-free biscotti. The resulting wet, gooey dough didn't work out for biscotti, but these moist chocolate delights were born.

CHOCOLATE PECAN COOKIES

24 pecan halves

2⅓ cups almond flour

½ cup unsweetened cocoa powder

½ teaspoon baking soda

⅛ teaspoon salt

½ cup vegetable oil

½ cup pure maple syrup

1. Preheat the oven to 350°F. Line a baking sheet with parchment paper.

2. Arrange the pecan halves on the baking sheet and toast them in the oven until slightly darker and aromatic, about 10 minutes. Remove from the baking sheet and cool completely. (Leave the oven on.)

3. In a large bowl, whisk together the almond flour, cocoa powder, baking soda, and salt. Stir in the oil and maple syrup and mix until everything is well combined.

4. Using a melon baller or teaspoon, drop teaspoons of the mixture 1 inch apart onto the baking sheet. Press a pecan half onto each cookie.

5. Bake the cookies until firm to the touch, 7 to 8 minutes. Allow to cool slightly on the pan before transferring to a wire rack.

McKenna Greenleaf Faulk
Los Angeles, California

McKenna Greenleaf Faulk is a student in the environmental magnet program at the Thomas Starr King Middle School in the Silver Lake section of Los Angeles. When a teacher tasked the 13-year-old and her classmates with a community service project, the teen knew fighting hunger was what she wanted to do. "I spearheaded an initiative to redistribute unused, packaged foods from the school cafeteria to local food pantries that serve the homeless," she says.

Except McKenna learned it wasn't quite so easy. A similar program elsewhere in Los Angeles failed when a homeless man was sickened by food that had not been kept at the proper temperature.

"I realized the solution was simply to refrigerate the food and to distribute it in coolers that maintain temperature," says the teen. The group called itself 37 Degrees from Hunger because 37°F is the ideal temperature at which food is safely stored in a refrigerator. "We are hoping this can be a blueprint for other kids at other schools," she says. "Even a kid can make a difference. And a lot of small programs together can make a big impact."

McKenna's **Pumpkin Chocolate Chip Cookies** are a holiday-season favorite of the Greenleaf Faulk family.

PUMPKIN CHOCOLATE
CHIP COOKIES

  1 cup vegetable oil

  2 eggs, beaten

  1 cup brown sugar

  1 cup granulated sugar

  1 teaspoon vanilla extract

3¾ cups canned pumpkin puree

  4 cups all-purpose flour

  2 teaspoons baking soda

  2 teaspoons ground cinnamon

  2 teaspoons ground ginger

  1 teaspoon ground allspice

  1 teaspoon freshly grated nutmeg

  1 teaspoon salt

  ½ teaspoon ground cloves

 12 ounces chocolate chips

1½ cups chopped walnuts (optional)

1. Preheat the oven to 350°F. Line a baking sheet with parchment paper.

2. In a large bowl, beat together the oil and eggs until combined. Add the two sugars and vanilla and mix well to combine. (Alternatively, you can do this in the bowl of a stand mixer and mix on low until well combined, about 2 minutes.) Stir in the pumpkin and mix until completely combined (about 1 minute in a stand mixer).

3. In another large bowl, whisk together the flour, baking soda, cinnamon, ginger, allspice, nutmeg, salt, and cloves. Add this mixture to the oil and pumpkin mixture in three batches, mixing thoroughly after each addition. The batter should be like very thick cake batter.

4. Stir in the chocolate chips and nuts (if using). Drop heaping tablespoons of the batter onto the baking sheet, leaving a little room around each cookie, although they will not spread much. This will need to be done in several batches.

5. Bake until the centers spring back when touched in the center, about 15 minutes. Cool on the baking sheet for 10 minutes.

Drusilla Rose Falco
Garden City, New York

"I am a firm believer that cakes and cookies and pies can change the world," says Dru Falco, who shares just exactly how that could be in a video on her blog *Teenage Cakeland*. The avid Long Island baker counts what she calls "the rush of learning a new technique or recipe" as "exhilarating," and that enthusiasm feeds her civic spirit as well. "Last year I set up a cupcake sale for She's the First, a nonprofit that helps girls in Third World countries receive an education," says Dru. "It felt so good to know that something that personally makes me so happy can help out girls around the world who are not as fortunate as I am."

Dru's **Classic Chocolate Cake with Speculoos Frosting** is iced with frosting made with speculoos cookie butter, a Belgian spread made from ground up Dutch shortbread cookies (called *speculoos*) and that tastes similar to dark caramel. Chocolate shards arranged on top of the finished cake create a dramatic look, but the cake is equally good without them.

(continued)

CLASSIC CHOCOLATE CAKE WITH SPECULOOS FROSTING

MAKES 1 LAYER CAKE (SERVES 12)

Cake

Baking spray

8 tablespoons (1 stick) butter

¼ cup applesauce

¼ cup vegetable oil

1½ cups brewed coffee

1 tablespoon vanilla extract

¾ cup unsweetened cocoa powder

2 cups granulated sugar

2 cups all-purpose flour

1½ teaspoons baking soda

½ teaspoon salt

⅔ cup sour cream or yogurt, at room temperature

2 eggs, at room temperature

Chocolate shard garnish

½ cup chopped semisweet chocolate or chocolate chips

Edible gold dust (optional)

Speculoos frosting

¾ pound (3 sticks) butter, at room temperature

1 cup speculoos cookie butter

⅓ cup milk

1 teaspoon ground cinnamon

½ teaspoon salt

½ teaspoon vanilla extract

6 cups powdered sugar, or more as needed to achieve correct consistency

1. For the cake: Preheat the oven to 350°F. Coat two 9-inch round cake pans with baking spray and then line with parchment paper rounds.

2. In a medium saucepan, melt the butter over medium heat. Whisk in the applesauce and vegetable oil, then the coffee, vanilla, and cocoa powder until smooth. Remove from the heat and set aside to cool slightly.

3. In a stand mixer fitted with the whisk, mix together the granulated sugar, flour, baking soda, and salt.

4. In a medium bowl, beat together the sour cream or yogurt and eggs until smooth.

5. Quickly pour a few tablespoons of the cocoa mixture into the egg mixture, while vigorously whisking, until the mixture is smooth. Pour the rest of the cocoa mixture into the egg mixture in a steady stream, whisking the whole time.

6. Make a well in the center of the dry ingredients and pour the egg-chocolate mixture into the center. Stir on low until no lumps remain.

7. Divide the batter between the cake pans and bake until a cake tester comes out clean, 25 to 30 minutes. Cool in the pans for 10 minutes then turn out of the pans onto wire racks to cool completely before decorating.

8. For the chocolate shard garnish: Line a 9 × 13-inch baking pan with wax paper or a silicone baking mat.

9. Place the chocolate pieces or chips in a small microwaveable bowl and microwave on 100% power in 20- to 30-second increments, stirring after each, until melted. Pour the melted chocolate onto the lined baking pan and spread thinly and evenly across the paper so that the chocolate is evenly distributed. Refrigerate the baking sheet for 15 to 20 minutes to set the chocolate.

10. Meanwhile, for the frosting: In a stand mixer, cream the butter for 2 minutes on medium-high speed. Add the cookie butter, milk, cinnamon, salt, and vanilla and cream on medium-high for an additional minute. On low speed, add the powdered sugar a little at a time, then increase the speed to medium-high for about 30 seconds. The frosting should have a thin, creamy consistency, so a knife placed in the center of the bowl will fall when the bowl is jiggled.

11. To assemble the cake, using a large serrated knife, slice the tops off the layers so they are flat. Place a dollop of frosting in the middle of a cake plate and position the first layer top-side down. Cut out several 10 × 4 inch strips of parchment paper and slide them under the cake layer to keep the plate clean.

12. Use about 1 cup of frosting and frost the bottom layer. Position the top layer on the first layer, top-side down. Frost the top layer and the sides using the remaining frosting.

13. Remove the baking sheet with the set chocolate from the refrigerator. Sprinkle lightly with a dusting of the edible gold, if using, then gently lift one end of the wax paper or silicone baking sheet. Using a table knife, tap the hardened chocolate in several places so it falls away from the sheet in large shards. Arrange these shards at standing angles on top of the cake.

14. Serve immediately or store, covered and refrigerated, for up to 1 week. If storing the cake, do not apply the chocolate shards and gold dust until just before serving.

Jess Dawson
Libertyville, Illinois

Little Jess Dawson's Easy-Bake Oven never had a chance. Even at 7 years old, the aspiring pastry chef was cranking out the desserts, giving the toy oven a workout it just couldn't handle. When it finally went kaput, Jess's mom suggested she move up to the real thing.

It was the beginning of a long career in food that would make most adult-chefs envious. At 14 she started interning with famed pastry chef Gale Gand, and by the time she was 16 she had a full-time job (when she wasn't in school) working with Gand and at Spiaggia, a Chicago restaurant.

Exuberant and cheerful, the now-18-year-old Jess seems like any other teenage girl, occupied with friends, school, and texting, but her culinary adventures include a Who's Who of American chefs. She's cooked at New York's James Beard House with chefs Rick Tramonto and John Folse, as well as appearing regularly with Chef Gand for cooking demos, food festivals, and other events.

"The exciting thing about food is that I have a million and two stories from it: places it's brought me, people I know and love because of it," says Jess, who now works at Chicago's Henri and interns at Grace Restaurant as well. "I never know where it's going to take me next!"

Food photography is yet another of Jess's passions and she posts her recipes and photos on *Livin' in the Kitchen,* her blog. She's always sure a new and exciting food experience is around the corner—and that's a feeling she wants to share with everyone.

"When I cook, I want people to remember the food," she says. "I want their first memory to be about how unbelievable the food was, their second to be who they ate it with, and their third to be how they got there."

Jess's **Banana Cake** is one of her signature mini desserts, but it can be made family-style as a square cake as well. Reminiscent of traditional banana bread with a more cake-like texture, the sweetness is balanced by the tang of the cream cheese frosting. Salted Caramel Drizzle—which is also delicious on Maple Butter Nut Ice Cream (page 243)—rounds out the cake luxuriously.

BANANA CAKE

Cake

Baking spray

2¼ cups sifted cake flour

¾ teaspoon baking soda

½ teaspoon baking powder

½ teaspoon salt

8 tablespoons (1 stick) butter, at room temperature

1½ cups sifted granulated sugar

2 eggs, at room temperature

1 cup ripe mashed banana

¼ cup vanilla yogurt or buttermilk, at room temperature

1 teaspoon vanilla extract

Frosting

10 ounces cream cheese, at room temperature

4 tablespoons (½ stick) butter, at room temperature

1 teaspoon vanilla extract

2 cups powdered sugar, sifted

Pinch of salt

Salted Caramel Drizzle (recipe follows)

1. For the cake: Preheat the oven to 350°F. Coat two 9 × 9-inch square cake pans with baking spray.

2. In a medium bowl, whisk together the flour, baking soda, baking powder, and salt.

3. In a stand mixer fitted with the paddle attachment, beat together the butter and granulated sugar until light and fluffy, 3 to 4 minutes. Add the eggs one at a time, mixing until totally combined.

4. In another bowl, mix together the banana, yogurt, and vanilla until well combined.

5. Add the flour mixture to the butter mixture in three parts, alternating with the banana mixture. Beat well after each addition until smooth.

6. Divide the batter between the 2 cake pans and bake until a cake tester inserted into the center of each pan comes out clean, about 45 minutes. Let the cakes cool completely in the pans.

7. Meanwhile, for the frosting: In a stand mixer fitted with the paddle attachment, beat together the cream cheese, butter, and vanilla until light and fluffy, 3 to 4 minutes. Gradually add the powdered sugar and salt, beating until smooth. Set aside.

8. To assemble the cakes, use a 3-inch round cookie cutter to cut out rounds of cake from each of the layers. Wipe the cookie cutter with a paper towel between cuts to ensure each cut-out is clean and sharp.

(continued)

9. Fit a piping bag with a #30 frosting tip and fill with the cream cheese frosting. Starting at the center of a cake round, pipe concentric circles of frosting, leaving about ¼ inch of cake edge unfrosted. Layer another cake round on top of the frosting and repeat the frosting process. Add a third cake layer and in the middle of this top layer, pipe a dollop of frosting onto the cake by squeezing the bag, then pipe frosting in concentric circles as you move the piping bag upward (think of a soft-serve ice cream cone). Drizzle with salted caramel sauce. Repeat the process for the remaining mini layer cakes.

10. Alternatively, you may frost the cake as a layer cake: Trim the top of each cake layer with a large, serrated knife to make each layer flat. Turn one layer upside down on a platter and frost the top with about half of the frosting. Carefully place the second layer face down on top of the first so that the bottom of this layer becomes the top of the cake. Frost the top and sides with the remaining frosting and then drizzle with caramel sauce.

Salted Caramel Drizzle

MAKES ABOUT 2 CUPS

This delightful caramel sauce gets its polish from the sea salt finish. Created by Jess Dawson for her banana cake, the sauce is equally good on ice cream or crepes or as a garnish for other frosted cakes.

1 cup sugar
7 tablespoons unsalted butter, cut into pieces, at room temperature
½ cup heavy cream, at room temperature
1½ teaspoons sea salt

1. In a heavy saucepan, melt ½ cup of the sugar over medium heat by swirling the pan until the sugar is melted.

2. Slowly add the remaining ½ cup sugar, 1 tablespoon at time, until all the sugar is melted. Stir with a wooden spoon until all the sugar has melted and is a dark amber color. Quickly add the butter, a few pieces at a time, stirring constantly.

3. Remove the saucepan from the heat and slowly whisk in the heavy cream until it is fully incorporated. Stir in the sea salt and allow the caramel drizzle to cool.

Amanda Koh Jia Yi
Singapore

A family obsession with commercially baked chocolate chip cookies is what pushed Amanda Yi into the kitchen. "I thought I could give chocolate chip cookies a shot," said 17-year-old Yi, who lives in Singapore. "I borrowed a book from the library for the recipe and, I remember, I didn't even know how to turn on the mixer!" Despite these handicaps, the cookies were a success and Amanda says she got hooked on the praise she received for her efforts. The result was a blog, *Crumbs and Cookies*, chronicling her adventures.

"If you knew me, you'd know my being a blogger is pretty funny because I'm a technology idiot," she laughs, pointing out that the actual baking is "90 percent of my life." Amanda says the most exciting thing about baking is seeing how a bunch of random ingredients can come together to form a dessert—particularly in layer cakes like this one, which has to be built in stages, with patience. "If you rush through the process you're not really enjoying it," she says. "I don't hurry when I bake. I always enter this Zen state at some point in the process and for a short blissful period of time I'm free of worries. It's like my mind is being shut off from the outside world."

Amanda's diminutive **Lemon White Chocolate & Strawberry Layer Cake** is so densely rich that a thin sliver is more than satisfying. It eschews the typical method of creaming butter and sugar in the cake batter and instead makes a "crumb" of flour and butter, which makes for a moister cake. The lemon curd frosting is so light in flavor and refreshing it works well with a variety of cake flavors— even chocolate. You'll find it addictive enough to keep in your regular frosting rotation.

Amanda makes this cake in a round mini pan, but a mini loaf pan works well too and is even readily available in disposable foil versions.

(continued)

LEMON WHITE CHOCOLATE & STRAWBERRY LAYER CAKE

Cake

Baking spray

¾ cup cake flour

½ cup sugar

1½ teaspoons baking powder

½ teaspoon salt

¾ cup (1½ sticks) unsalted butter

⅓ cup milk

2 egg whites

¾ teaspoon vanilla extract

White chocolate filling

1½ ounces white chocolate, chopped

½ cup heavy (whipping) cream

Lemon curd

Grated zest of 1½ lemons

½ cup sugar

2 large eggs

¼ cup plus 2 tablespoons fresh lemon juice

10½ tablespoons unsalted butter, diced, at room temperature

1 pint strawberries, sliced

1. For the cake: Preheat the oven to 300°F. Line a 5 × 2-inch round cake pan with a round of parchment and lightly coat the paper with baking spray.

2. In a stand mixer fitted with the paddle attachment, on low speed, mix together the cake flour, sugar, baking powder, and salt. Add the butter and continue beating on low speed until the mixture resembles moist crumbs.

3. In a separate bowl, whisk together the milk, egg whites, and vanilla. Add all but 3 table-spoons of this mixture to the flour mixture and beat on medium speed for 1½ minutes. Add the remaining milk mixture and beat for 30 seconds more. Using a rubber spatula, scrape down the sides of the bowl and mix on medium speed for another 20 seconds.

4. Pour the batter into the prepared pan and bake until a cake tester comes out mostly clean, with moist crumbs attached, 30 to 40 minutes.

5. Meanwhile, for the white chocolate filling: In a small saucepan over low heat, combine the white chocolate and 2 tablespoons of the heavy cream. Stir constantly until the white chocolate melts. Remove the pan from the heat and set aside to cool completely.

6. In a stand mixer with the whisk attachment, whip the remaining heavy cream until it forms medium peaks, about 3 minutes. Add the cooled white chocolate mixture and whip until the cream forms stiff peaks, about 2 minutes more. Set aside.

7. For the lemon curd: Place the lemon zest and sugar in a large heatproof bowl and rub the two together until the sugar is moist, grainy, and aromatic. Whisk in the eggs and lemon juice.

8. Place the bowl over a large saucepan of simmering water and cook, whisking constantly, until the mixture thickens and reaches 180°F. Immediately remove from heat and strain the lemon mixture into the bowl of a stand mixer fitted with the paddle attachment. Let the mixture cool to 140°F, stirring occasionally.

9. When the mixture has cooled to 140°F, start adding the butter 4 or 5 pieces at a time, beating on high speed to incorporate before adding more. When all the butter has been incorporated, beat the curd for another 3 to 4 minutes. Scrape the curd into a bowl and refrigerate until firm, at least 4 hours.

10. To assemble the cake, trim the top of the cake so that it is flat, then slice the cake horizontally into 3 layers. Place the top layer face down on a cake plate. Spread half the white chocolate filling on the top of this layer. Lightly layer with half the strawberries. Top with the second layer of cake and spread the remaining white chocolate filling on top and the remaining strawberries. Finish with the last layer of cake and refrigerate it until the white chocolate filling is firm, about 2 hours.

11. Frost the top and sides of the chilled cake with the lemon curd.

Sasha Meshcherekova
Vancouver, British Columbia, Canada

Cooking is the way Canadian teen Sasha Meshcherekova bonds with her friends. "We are always cooking together, sharing recipes, and asking each other advice," says the 14-year-old.

Attending culinary camp last summer with a pal was a formative experience in her cooking life because of the advanced techniques and flavor combinations that she learned there. "We did a Master Chef–style mystery box competition and I got to be captain of my team," says Sasha. "It taught me teamwork and how to divide and conquer a dish in a certain time limit."

That spirit of culinary cooperation is a recurring theme on her blog *Teen Chef in the Kitchen*, which features projects with her dad and friends.

Sasha's **Strawberry-Basil Cupcakes** started out with a base cake recipe provided by a foodie friend to which she added basil, which adds a delicate, minty flavor.

STRAWBERRY-BASIL CUPCAKES

MAKES 1 DOZEN

Cupcakes

- 1 cup milk
- 1 teaspoon apple cider vinegar
- 1/3 cup canola oil
- 3/4 cup granulated sugar
- 2 teaspoons vanilla extract
- 1 1/3 cups all-purpose flour
- 3/4 teaspoon baking powder
- 1/2 teaspoon baking soda
- 1/4 teaspoon salt
- 1 cup diced strawberries
- 1 tablespoon chopped fresh basil

Frosting

- 8 ounces cream cheese
- 4 tablespoons (1/2 stick) butter
- 1/2 teaspoon vanilla extract
- 1/8 teaspoon mint extract
- 2 1/2 to 2 3/4 cups powdered sugar
- 2 to 3 teaspoons chopped fresh basil
- 1 tablespoon chopped fresh mint

(continued)

1. For the cupcakes: Preheat the oven to 350°F. Line 12 cups of a muffin tin with paper liners.

2. In a medium bowl, combine the milk and vinegar and set aside for 5 minutes or until the milk curdles. Then stir in the oil, granulated sugar, and vanilla.

3. In a large bowl, whisk together the flour, baking powder, baking soda, and salt. Add the milk mixture to the flour mixture and beat until smooth. Fold in the strawberries and basil.

4. Fill the muffin cups two-thirds of the way. Bake until a cake tester comes out clean, 20 to 25 minutes. Remove from the oven and cool completely before frosting.

5. For the frosting: In a bowl, with an electric mixer, cream the cream cheese and butter until light and fluffy, about 2 minutes. Beat in the vanilla and mint extracts until well combined. Gradually beat in the powdered sugar until combined. Fold in the basil and the mint.

6. Frost the tops of the cooled cupcakes with the frosting.

Eeshan Chakrabarti
Lincolnshire, Illinois

According to his mother, 9-year-old Eeshan Chakrabarti was such a picky eater that mealtime was more like a declaration of war. It was getting the youngster into the kitchen and in front of a stove that turned the tides. Eeshan has graduated to assisting his father at the grill (and is unafraid to take Dad to task if the meat isn't done perfectly) and has made the Italian dessert **Tiramisu** his specialty. "I want to make food better and better," he says. "That way people will enjoy it more." Rum provides an integral part of this flavor profile and tiramisu is best when the flavors are allowed to mellow together. If you can allow it to sit overnight, then do so.

TIRAMISU

SERVES 8 TO 10

6 large pasteurized egg yolks, at room temperature

¼ cup sugar

½ cup rum

1½ cups brewed espresso

16 ounces mascarpone cheese, at room temperature

24 savoiardo (Italian ladyfingers)

¼ cup powdered sugar

¼ cup unsweetened cocoa powder

1. In a large bowl, using a hand mixer, whisk the egg yolks and sugar on high. Place the bowl over a saucepan of simmering water and continue to mix on medium speed until the yolks double in volume (4 to 5 minutes).

2. Lower the speed to medium and add ¼ cup of the rum, ¼ cup of the espresso, and the mascarpone. Whisk until smooth, 1 to 2 minutes.

3. In a shallow bowl, combine the remaining ¼ cup rum and 1¼ cups espresso. Dip 1 side of half of the ladyfingers in the espresso/rum mixture and line the bottom of a 9 × 12 × 2-inch dish. Pour half the espresso cream mixture evenly on top. Dip 1 side of the remaining ladyfingers in the espresso/rum mixture and place them in a second layer on top of the espresso cream.

4. Pour the rest of the espresso cream over the top of the second layer and smooth it. Cover with plastic wrap and refrigerate for 4 to 6 hours or, ideally, overnight.

5. Remove plastic wrap and dust the tiramisu with powdered sugar and cocoa powder.

Daniel Hamilton
Toronto, Ontario, Canada

Daniel Hamilton made his first full meal at age 6, surprising his mother, Sandra, so much that she videotaped an encore of the young cook in action—just to prove to others that it really happened. The response was so great among family and friends that the duo continued to film Daniel's kitchen escapades. They posted the videos on a YouTube channel and website called *Quite a Bite*, ultimately earning the 11-year-old a spot on Food Network's *Rachael vs. Guy: Kids Cook-Off* cooking show.

"I was the only kid from Canada on the show!" says Daniel, who admits he thought it was a long shot when he submitted his audition tape to the American television network.

The appearance earned Daniel fame in his native Toronto where, he says, he's been recognized on the street and even asked for autographs. He continues to share his skills through cooking demonstrations and appearances in local schools including the one where his mom is a teacher. "My mom said that after I visited for Career Day I had inspired a few students to cook and watch my YouTube videos for more pointers," he says. "That made me happy that something I love so much can touch so many people!"

Daniel's **Superfruit Crumble** earned him points with the judges when he appeared on *Rachael vs. Guy*. Much of the sweetness of this dish comes from the fruit. Fresh seasonal berries are best for this dish, but organic frozen berries can work well too. Vanilla yogurt serves as a healthy topping for the crumble, but a little vanilla ice cream would be lovely (if more indulgent!) too.

SUPERFRUIT CRUMBLE

1½ cups blueberries

1½ cups strawberries, cut into small pieces

3 small plums, pitted and cut into small pieces

1 peach, pitted and cut into small pieces

1 tablespoon granulated sugar

1 to 2 teaspoons ground cinnamon

1 teaspoon ground allspice

2 cups all-purpose flour

1 cup brown sugar

½ pound (2 sticks) butter, melted

½ cup vanilla Greek yogurt

1. Preheat the oven to 350°F. Butter six ¾-cup ramekins and place on a baking sheet.

2. Put the fruits in a large bowl and add the granulated sugar, cinnamon, and allspice. Mix lightly so that all the fruit is coated. Set aside.

3. In a large bowl, mix together the flour and brown sugar. Stir in the melted butter and mix until the mixture is crumbly.

4. Divide the fruit mixture among the ramekins, leave enough space at the top of each for the crumble. Divide the crumble mixture equally among the ramekins.

5. Bake until the crumble is golden brown and the berries are bubbling, 20 to 30 minutes. Serve warm with vanilla yogurt on top of each.

Tyler Trainer
Windermere, Florida

Tyler Trainer's mom, Lori, says his considerable cooking skills are a family mystery since neither she nor his dad cook. But it's a welcome mystery for the family who benefits from the 16-year-old's efforts. Baking is Tyler's specialty and when he was 10 he made a Key lime pie for his dad's birthday and then again for a neighbor's party. He later got so many requests for the confection that with his dad's help, he started his own company: Pie in the Sky Bakery. Tyler says learning to cook—and particularly to bake—has always been his dream, though sometimes folks don't take him seriously because he's a kid. He also struggles to prove to his friends that baking is a guy's game. "Many kids my age think baking is 'girly.' I don't think that is true. Just look at Duff Goldman, Guy Fieri, Bobby Flay, and many other people on television," says Tyler. Even though Tyler creates all kinds of special-occasion cakes and pies—he recently made a Hello Kitty graduation cake—his **Key Lime Pie** is his standout signature favorite. The pie's whipped cream topping adds a refreshing finish to the balanced sweet and tangy filling. It's the fresh Key lime juice, says Tyler, that's the key to making this simple pie superior.

(continued)

Limes

Limes are a citrus fruit that offer flavor far beyond simply sour. Happily, a far wider variety of limes are now available in gourmet and specialty markets including the Key limes called for in Tyler Trainer's Key Lime Pie. Key limes are a smaller version of the fruit and are not much larger than a gumball. Kalamansis (aka calamondin), citrus fruits that are only called limes because they are often sold while their skins are still green, are used abundantly in the Philippines. Kalamansis are slightly smaller than average supermarket limes (Persian limes) and have a yellow-orange flesh when ripe. They are somewhat sweeter too. Kalamansi lime juice would be an excellent substitute for the lemon juice in Marshall Bennett's Grilled Caribbasian Citrus Chicken (page 145). Kaffir limes, which are a staple in Thai cooking, are about the size of golf balls and have a dimpled flesh. They are prized equally for their aroma as their juice. Try kaffir lime juice in Amber Kelley's Refreshing Thai Cucumber Salad (page 19).

KEY LIME PIE

Crust

14 cinnamon graham crackers or 1 cup graham cracker crumbs

1 tablespoon sugar

5 tablespoons unsalted butter, melted

Filling

4 egg yolks

½ cup fresh Key lime juice

1 can (14 ounces) sweetened condensed milk

Topping

1 cup heavy (whipping) cream

2 tablespoons powdered sugar

½ teaspoon vanilla extract

Lime zest, for garnish

1. For the crust: Preheat the oven to 325°F.

2. Break the graham crackers into large pieces and grind them in a food processor until they reach the consistency of coarse flour. Pour into a large bowl and mix in the sugar. Stir in the melted butter. It should be the consistency of wet sand. Press this mixture into a 9-inch pie pan and bake for 15 minutes to set. Remove from the oven to cool completely. (Leave the oven on.)

3. For the filling: In a large bowl, beat together the egg yolks, lime juice, and condensed milk until well combined.

4. Pour the lime mixture into the pie crust. Bake until the mixture is firm (but not browned), about 20 minutes. Let the pie cool completely, then refrigerate for at least 8 hours or, preferably, overnight.

5. For the topping: In a large bowl, with an electric mixer, combine the cream, powdered sugar, and vanilla and whip on high until stiff peaks form (3 to 5 minutes with a handheld mixer, 2 minutes in a stand mixer).

6. Spread the whipped cream over the pie just before serving. Garnish with lime zest.

Justin G. Goodwin
Far Rockaway, New York

The chance to explore the world through food is one of the most exciting things about cooking for 12-year-old Justin Goodwin, who lives in the borough of Queens in New York City. Justin, who says he learned to cook from both his mom and from Food Network, plans to one day be a professional chef with an equally savory and sweet repertoire. This **Maple Butter Nut Ice Cream's** heavy egg base makes it more like a custard or even a churned crème brûlée.

MAPLE BUTTER NUT ICE CREAM MAKES 1 QUART

8 tablespoons (1 stick) butter

2½ cups heavy (whipping) cream

½ cup milk

2 teaspoons vanilla extract

6 egg yolks

1 cup brown sugar

Salt

1½ cups chopped walnuts

¼ cup maple syrup

1. In a small saucepan, melt the butter over medium-low heat. Cook the butter until it turns a deep golden brown, 4 to 5 minutes. Remove from the heat and set aside.

2. In a medium saucepan, combine the cream, milk, and vanilla and heat over medium heat until they just come to a boil, about 3 minutes. Set aside.

3. In a stand mixer fitted with the paddle attachment, combine the egg yolks, brown sugar, and ½ teaspoon salt and beat until fluffy, scraping down the sides of the bowl with a rubber spatula once or twice, 8 to 9 minutes. Slowly pour the melted butter into the egg mixture while mixing on medium speed. When completely combined, slowly add the cream mixture and mix until totally combined.

4. Pour the mixture back into the medium saucepan over low heat and cook slowly, stirring, until the mixture thickly coats the back of a spoon, 5 to 6 minutes. Remove from the heat and pour into a bowl to cool. Refrigerate the mixture until it is completely cold.

5. Meanwhile, in a large skillet, toss the walnuts with ⅛ teaspoon salt and cook over medium-low heat, stirring often, until aromatic and toasted, about 3 minutes. Stir in the maple syrup and mix to coat the walnuts completely. Remove from the heat.

6. Pour the milk mixture into the chilled bowl of an ice cream machine and churn according to manufacturer's directions until doubled in volume and firm. Add the maple walnuts to the ice cream in the last 10 minutes of its churn cycle.

7. Scoop the ice cream into a quart container, seal, and freeze for at least 4 hours before serving.

Mason Estrada
Rockwall, Texas

"I love the idea that I can make something new and exciting every day," says Mason Estrada, a high school junior in Texas. "I wake up every morning and get to create and innovate. How many people get to do that on a daily basis?"

Creative in other fields as well, when Mason isn't enjoying the magic of cooking he performs actual magic tricks and is a 3D artist and sculptor who has entered statewide competitions.

Mason counts his contribution of a recipe to a healthy cookbook for kids, produced by the Children's Medical Center of Dallas, among the most important things he's done with food to date.

"My greatest aspiration is to open my own restaurant," he says. "But before I do that I absolutely must travel the country and the world learning about different kinds of foods and preparation methods."

The young cook's **Sweet Potato Ice Cream** exemplifies his style of cooking with what he calls "simple yet bold" flavors. Sweet potatoes are a popular tuber in Mason's native Texas in a number of sweet and savory preparations and the inspiration for this dish.

SWEET POTATO ICE CREAM

1 small sweet potato, peeled and cut into chunks

1¼ cups heavy (whipping) cream

½ cup whole milk

½ cup brown sugar

⅛ teaspoon freshly grated nutmeg

½ teaspoon ground cinnamon

3 egg yolks

1. In a small saucepan, bring 2 cups of water to a boil and add the sweet potato. Reduce the heat to a simmer and cook the sweet potato until tender, 25 to 30 minutes. Drain the sweet potato chunks, transfer to a blender or food processor, and puree until smooth.

2. In a medium saucepan, whisk together the heavy cream, milk, brown sugar, nutmeg, and cinnamon over medium heat until the sugar is dissolved and the mixture just comes to a boil, about 3 minutes. Remove from the heat.

3. In a large bowl, whisk the egg yolks and slowly pour the hot cream into the yolks in a thin stream. When all the cream mixture is combined with the yolks, return the whole mixture to the saucepan over medium-low heat.

4. Cook the egg mixture, whisking constantly until it thickens enough to thickly coat the back of a spoon, 4 to 5 minutes. Whisk in the sweet potato puree until combined.

5. Pour the sweet potato mixture into a bowl and refrigerate until completely cold.

6. Pour the mixture into the chilled bowl of an ice cream maker and churn according to manufacturer's directions until doubled in volume and firm. Scrape ice cream into a 1-quart freezer container and freeze for 2 more hours for a firmer ice cream.

Abbie Emmons
Wells, Vermont

Seventeen-year-old Abbie Emmons first got inspired to start cooking when she learned that many premade, processed foods could be made from scratch with real, healthful ingredients.

"I've learned so much in just these past few years about the importance of eating whole foods, and beyond that, eating organic and non-GMO foods," she says. "It has really changed my life."

Yet, even though she was cooking from scratch, Abbie says, her repertoire was initially based on using refined sugar, butter, and white flour. "One day, my mom approached me with a dare—to bake only foods that are healthy for us, or don't bake anything at all," she says. "I began to research the ingredients I was using and quickly started to discover that there are many healthy substitutions available."

Abbie uses whole wheat flour and unrefined coconut oil in her **Gingerbread Waffles.** While the waffles are not particularly sweet, the roasted pear topping adds exactly the right note of balanced sweetness.

GINGERBREAD WAFFLES WITH ROASTED PEAR TOPPING

SERVES 4

Waffles

½ cup whole wheat flour

½ cup pastry flour

½ teaspoon baking powder

½ teaspoon baking soda

½ teaspoon salt

1 teaspoon ground cinnamon

½ teaspoon ground ginger

¼ teaspoon ground allspice

⅛ teaspoon ground cloves

2 large eggs, separated

3 tablespoons coconut oil, melted and cooled

½ cup coconut milk

¼ cup sour cream

3 tablespoons unsulfured molasses

Roasted pears

Cooking spray

2 large Bosc pears, cored and roughly chopped

1 teaspoon ground cinnamon

⅓ cup pecans, chopped into small pieces

Maple syrup, for serving

Vanilla ice cream, for serving

1. Preheat the oven to 400°F.

2. For the waffles: In a large bowl, whisk together the flours, baking powder, baking soda, salt, cinnamon, ginger, allspice, and cloves. Set aside.

3. In a bowl, with an electric mixer, beat the egg whites on high speed until soft peaks begin to form (5 to 6 minutes with a hand-held mixer, 3 to 4 minutes with a stand mixer). Set aside.

4. In another bowl, whisk together the egg yolks, melted coconut oil, coconut milk, sour cream, and molasses until well combined. Add the flour mixture to the molasses mixture, whisking until smooth. Gently fold the whipped egg whites into this batter with a rubber spatula. Do not overmix. Set aside.

5. For the roasted pears: Coat a 2-quart baking dish with cooking spray and layer in the pears. Sprinkle with cinnamon and pecans. Roast until the pears are fork-tender and beginning to caramelize, 25 to 30 minutes. Remove and let cool for 5 minutes.

6. While the pears are baking, heat a waffle iron to medium-high. Scoop about ½ cup of batter evenly into the center of the waffle iron. Cook according to the manufacturer's directions until browned and fluffy. Repeat with the remaining batter.

7. To serve, top each waffle with an equal amount of pears and pecans. Drizzle with maple syrup and, if desired, top with a scoop of vanilla ice cream.

Brandon Scawthorn
Kyle, Texas

At 11 years old, Texas native Brandon Scawthorn has already been the winner of a national cooking show and a competitive motocross racer. A home video, taken on his father's iPhone, earned the young cook a place on Food Network's *Rachael vs. Guy: Kids Cook-Off*, which he ultimately won.

"All the competitors were older. Many had their own cooking web series. One had cooked for the First Lady. Two had acting agents and one had a best-selling book," he says. "I only had cooking experience with my mom. Some were nervous. I was not. Some were overconfident. I was not. But my mom was with me, so I was happy." Brandon went on to win the contest with a Korean-style rib recipe he learned from a Korean neighbor and that he adapted to make his own.

The youngster, who attends a magnet school that focuses on Science, Technology, Engineering and Math (STEM), says that it's motorcycle racing that has taught him to keep his cool.

"I am rarely nervous. I am used to competing at 70 mph in 115°F temperatures—knowing I could wreck at any time," he says. "Taking a test or speaking in front of people is easy by comparison."

True to his word, he wasn't even nervous when he taught fellow-guest Regis Philbin his **Crepes with Sweet Cream & Berries** recipe on the nationally televised *Rachael Ray Show* in 2013. Make this extremely versatile recipe by creating your own mix of fruits. Salted Caramel Drizzle (page 230) also makes a nice garnish for the finished crepes.

(continued)

CREPES WITH SWEET CREAM & BERRIES

Crepes

2 eggs

⅛ teaspoon salt

1 teaspoon vanilla extract

⅓ cup sugar

5 heaping tablespoons all-purpose flour

½ cup milk, or more as needed

Cooking spray or melted butter, for the griddle

3 tablespoons powdered sugar, for dusting

Sauce

2 tablespoons butter

½ cup sugar

2 tablespoons kirschwasser, framboise, or Grand Marnier

1 tablespoon cornstarch

3 cups assorted summer fruits, such as sliced strawberries, blackberries, raspberries, blueberries, and halved cherries

1 teaspoon vanilla extract

Juice of ½ lemon

Filling

8 ounces farmer's cheese

¼ to ⅓ cup sugar (to taste)

1 teaspoon vanilla extract

3 to 6 tablespoons heavy (whipping) cream or sour cream

Whipped cream

1 cup heavy (whipping) cream

1 tablespoon powdered sugar

1. For the crepes: In a bowl, whisk together the eggs, salt, vanilla, and sugar. Whisk in the flour and a small amount of the milk. Continue whisking in just enough milk to make a batter that is the consistency of heavy cream. Set aside.

2. For the sauce: In a 4-quart saucepan, melt the butter over medium-high heat and add the sugar. Cook, stirring, until the sugar is melted. In a small bowl, combine ½ cup water, the fruit liqueur, and cornstarch and stir until well blended. Add to the butter mixture and cook over medium-low heat until thickened slightly, about 1 minute. Add the fruit, bring the mixture to a simmer, and cook until thickened, 3 to 5 minutes. Remove the pan from the heat and stir in the vanilla and lemon juice. Set aside.

3. For the filling: In medium bowl, with an electric mixer, beat together the farmer's cheese, sugar, vanilla, and enough of the heavy cream or sour cream to achieve a smooth, thick filling. Set aside.

4. For the whipped cream: In a large bowl, with an electric mixer, beat together the cream and powdered sugar until the mixture holds stiff peaks (4 to 5 minutes with a handheld mixer, 3 to 4 minutes in a stand mixer). Set aside.

5. To make the crepes, heat a large skillet or a griddle over medium-high heat and coat with cooking spray or brush with melted butter. Pour ¼ cup of batter into the center of the skillet or griddle and, using the back of a spoon, gently make concentric circles from the center of the batter outward, pushing the batter into a wider circle as you go. Cook until the crepe is lightly browned, 2 to 3 minutes. Do not flip over. Remove and keep warm. Repeat until all the batter is used up.

6. To assemble the crepes, place a crepe, browned-side down, on a plate. Spoon 1 tablespoon of filling on one side of the crepe and roll the crepe forward over the filling into a tight cylinder. Repeat until all the crepes are filled. Place 2 crepes in the center of each plate and spoon 2 to 3 tablespoons of the warm fruit sauce over the crepes. Top with the whipped cream and dust with the powdered sugar. Serve immediately.

Mia Jessurun
Sydney, New South Wales, Australia

Inspired at age 10 by a teacher who was a Buddhist and a vegetarian and later by a classmate who participated in meatless Mondays, Mia Jessurun says that once upon a time being a vegetarian made her unique. "Now a lot of kids are vegetarians, so I'm not that different. But that's a good thing!" she says.

A seminal event in the teen's path away from animal proteins came on a family trip to Thailand where they ordered prawns at a local restaurant. "They came to the table alive, jumping about under the plate cover," she says. "I don't remember much after that, but I do remember a lot of crying and being totally put off prawns."

Mia says that being a vegetarian has encouraged her to use the skills taught her by her mom, who is a professionally trained chef. She often cooks her own vegetarian meals and desserts because she doesn't feel her vegetarian lifestyle should dictate the other cooking in the family kitchen.

Her **Chocolate Apple Chia Seed Pudding** uses chia seeds for an extra level of creaminess and protein. Mia blogs about her cooking adventures on *The Little Blue Bicycle*.

CHOCOLATE APPLE CHIA SEED PUDDING

SERVES 4

1 cup low-fat milk
2 tablespoons brown sugar
2 tablespoons white chia seeds
¼ cup unsweetened cocoa powder
½ teaspoon ground cinnamon
1 small apple, peeled and grated
1 tablespoon dried currants

1. In a food processor, combine the milk, brown sugar, chia seeds, cocoa powder, and cinnamon. Blend until smooth, about 2 minutes. Stir in the grated apple and mix well.

2. Pour the mixture into 4 small bowls or ramekins. Top each pudding with currants and seal tightly with plastic wrap.

3. Refrigerate until set, about 2 hours.

Logan Bello
Sebastopol, California

Logan Bello is determined to teach other kids that it's not all that difficult to make something homemade. A participant in several cooking contests and a demo at national Food Day at his school, Logan says the great thing about his **Panna Cotta** recipe is that it's far simpler than the impressive end-result makes it seem. "You can also make these in advance," he says. "Just keep them well covered and well chilled." Gelatin is used to thicken this light pudding, which makes it a *panna cotta* rather than a *crème* or traditional pudding, which uses egg yolks . The lightness of the panna cotta provides just enough of a creamy counterpoint to the raspberries. Strawberries are a nice substitution for the raspberries as well.

PANNA COTTA   SERVES 8

  4 cups heavy (whipping) cream
 ½ cup sugar
  1 vanilla bean, split lengthwise
4½ teaspoons unflavored gelatin
    Cooking spray
    Fresh raspberries, for garnish
    Small mint leaves, for garnish

1. In a medium saucepan, combine the heavy cream and sugar. Using a paring knife, scrape the seeds out of the vanilla bean and add them and the pod to the cream and sugar. Heat the cream mixture over medium heat, whisking until the sugar is dissolved. Remove from the heat, cover the saucepan, and set aside 30 minutes to allow the vanilla bean to infuse the cream mixture.

2. Remove the vanilla bean pods and return the saucepan to medium heat. Bring to just under a boil. Remove from the heat and set aside.

3. Meanwhile, measure ¼ cup plus 2 tablespoons cold water into a medium bowl. Sprinkle the gelatin over the cold water and let stand 5 to 10 minutes or until it blooms.

4. Pour the hot cream mixture over the gelatin and whisk until the gelatin is completely dissolved.

5. Lightly coat eight ¾-cup ramekins with cooking spray. Divide the panna cotta mixture evenly among the ramekins and chill until firm, at least 4 hours but, ideally, overnight.

6. To serve, run a sharp paring knife around the inside edge of each panna cotta and unmold each onto a serving plate. Garnish with fresh raspberries and a mint leaf.

CHAPTER 8

Sipz

(Beverages)

Whether it's a smoothie that eats a like a meal or simple refreshing drink, what's clear about the recipes in this chapter is that young chefs take their drinks as seriously as they take their food. Not an afterthought, a good beverage is instead the opportunity to explore different aspects of taste and texture. In each of these drinks you'll find the same attention to quality ingredients and detailed technique as well the hallmark values of the cooks of the next generation: vegan options, the use of whole, pure foods, and a toast-worthy belief in the power of produce as an access point to health. Here's looking at you, kids!

KEY: **GF** Gluten Free   **VG** Vegan   **V** Vegetarian

Koa Halpern
Denver, Colorado

Anti-fast food crusader, Koa Halpern advocates fresh, whole, organic, and raw ingredients. The vegetarian cook says his naturally sweet **Banana-Berry Smoothie** will wipe out any junk food cravings because of its nutritional density—it's chock-full of nutrients from the dairy (calcium) and flaxseed oil (omega-3s). For more about Koa and his Fast Food Free campaign, see page 191.

BANANA-BERRY SMOOTHIE   SERVES 2

½ banana, frozen
½ cup rice milk
½ cup blueberry coconut yogurt
2 cups frozen mixed berries
¼ cup frozen orange juice concentrate
2 tablespoons flaxseed oil
1 tablespoon honey
4 ice cubes

Combine all the ingredients in a blender and puree until smooth and thick.

Jade Serenity Cruz
Spring Mills, Pennsylvania

Jade Cruz remembers serving meals at the local Salvation Army when she was just 7 years old, alongside her mom, whose beautiful smile offered comfort and encouragement to those who needed it most. When Jade's mother died 2 years ago, the then-10-year-old Jade left her Florida home to live with the father she barely knew in Pennsylvania. It was a hard transition, but made easier by the encouragement of her aunt Leslie with whom she lives as well.

It was at her aunt's Common Ground organic farm that Jade was able to explore her taste for whole food ingredients. "People said I was a picky eater, but I just don't like a lot of the processed foods that are out there," says the tween, who has never developed a taste for fast food. "I guess people eat them because that's what's available. Making your own food gives you more options."

Throwing herself into the activities on the farm helped Jade cope with her loss and taught her, in more ways than one, how to make lemonade from the lemons life may toss you. Last year, Jade set up an organic lemonade stand for the local organic FarmFest and served hundreds of eco-cups of her libation. She says it is a logical evolution of a kid's party drink called "Candy Soup" that she was famous for back home in Florida. "It wasn't very healthy, but kids loved it," she says. "My organic lemonade is much better." Jade sells her **Organic Festival Lemonade** at her local farmers' market on Saturdays throughout the summer.

Fresh seasonal fruit adds sweet brightness to the tart lemonade and Jade suggests using what's in season and looks best, or when out of season to use frozen organic fruit. Her original recipe calls for berries and watermelon, but other sweet melons or seasonal stone fruits like peaches and plums work incredibly well too.

ORGANIC FESTIVAL LEMONADE

1 cup freshly squeezed organic lemon juice

4¼ cups spring water or purified water

½ cup cut-up organic fruit such as watermelon, raspberries, or sliced strawberries (optional)

½ to ¾ cup organic sugar

6 organic lemon slices or orange slices

1. First make the lemon juice ice cubes 1 day ahead. Mix ½ cup of the lemon juice and ¼ cup of the spring water together and pour into an ice tray. Freeze overnight.

2. To make the lemonade, pour the remaining ½ cup lemon juice (and fresh fruit, if using) into a 1-quart canning jar. Add the sugar, using a little more than you might in order to counteract the tartness of the lemon juice ice cubes. Pour in the remaining spring water. Do not fill the jar to the rim, leave about ½ inch of space from the top of the liquid to the rim of the jar.

3. Tighten the lid of the canning jar and shake really well until the sugar is dissolved. Add the lemon or orange slices to the jar, and allow to sit for 15 minutes.

4. Place 3 or 4 lemon juice ice cubes into each of 4 glasses. Pour the lemonade over the ice cubes and spoon slices of fruit into the glasses as well, if desired.

Sadie Hope-Gund
New York, New York

Sadie Hope-Gund, 16, is the second half of the best-friend duo who star in *What's On Your Plate?*, a documentary by filmmaker (and Sadie's mom) Catherine Gund that follows the girls on their journey to understand where food really comes from as they explore issues from food deserts to factory farming. The documentary—which premiered at the Berlin International Film Festival in 2009 and was aired on the Discovery Channel—came about when Sadie, faced with genetically high cholesterol, had to either go on medication or change her entire way of eating.

Her predicament prompted the then 12-year-old Sadie to start asking questions about the nature of food and why it made some people sick. "I asked my mom why some people eat so much junk food and she said they don't always know the healthier option or why they should choose it," said Sadie. "Trying to crack that question was how *What's On Your Plate?* was born. We decided to explore where food comes from, what is in it, and how it affects children and families." In the film, Sadie and her best friend Safiyah Riddle interview farmers, nutritionists, politicians, community organizers, chefs, and families with kids suffering from diabetes and obesity-related illnesses.

Today Sadie's cholesterol is under control, thanks to the healthy recipes she has come to love, among them her **Blueberry-Almond Smoothie**. "This is one of my go-to snacks for all times of year, and all times of day! It is super-easy and quick," she says. "A little tweak of the ingredients, if you are feeling adventurous, can lead to a whole new smoothie." Try substituting cashews for the almonds in this recipe and a mix of raspberries and blackberries for the blueberries for an entirely different, yet equally delicious, flavor profile.

BLUEBERRY-ALMOND SMOOTHIE

MAKE 1 LARGE OR 2 SMALL SMOOTHIES

½ cup mango juice

¼ cup raw (skin-on) almonds

½ cup almond milk

1 banana

¼ cup blueberries

1 scoop whey protein powder

Combine all the ingredients in a powerful blender and pulse until smooth, about 1 minute. Add more mango juice, if needed to achieve a smoothie consistency. Serve cold.

John Breitfelder
New Canaan, Connecticut

Ever willing to experiment with new things, 10-year-old John Breitfelder is always looking for ways to incorporate the new ingredients he's learned about with old favorites. He fell in love with a smoothie at a new farm-to-table market in New Canaan, Connecticut, where he lives. After a little investigation he learned that they used agave syrup, which he had never tried before. " I decided to try my own combinations of fruit smoothies using agave," says John. "Mangoes are one of my favorite fruits and I've found they are delicious in smoothies." And so his **Mighty Mango Madness Smoothie** was born.

MIGHTY MANGO MADNESS SMOOTHIE

MAKES 1 LARGE SMOOTHIE

1 cup frozen mango pieces
3 strawberries, hulled
½ cup low-fat vanilla yogurt
1 teaspoon agave syrup
¼ cup water

Combine all the ingredients in a blender and puree until smooth.

Vanessa Arnold
Chicago, Illinois

It was Vanessa Arnold's older sister who pushed her into joining the After School Matters program when she was in seventh grade. The program, working in concert with Chicago Public Schools, offers teens a way to explore their talents in everything from creative writing, painting, and dance to the culinary arts—the area that captured Vanessa's interest. She remained with the program for 3 years, ultimately becoming a class leader and teaching cooking techniques to her peers.

"I was always the tall, chunky kid. The one who got made fun of," says Vanessa, who is now 17. "After School Matters became my escape from everything. My instructors opened my eyes and mind to many new things and ideas. I was exposed to the great world of food and kids who shared my passion."

Through the program Vanessa says she was able to take part in culinary competitions and speak publicly about how the program changed her life. In 2011, she and a team of five other students competed in the Cooking Up Change challenge hosted yearly by Chicago's nonprofit Healthy Schools Campaign, which advocates for healthy school environments for all children regardless of income or social status. That year Vanessa's team scored second place and then secured the top spot in 2012. With the win, each student in the team earned a $1,000 scholarship and a trip to Washington, DC, to be part of a national competition against seven other teams, where they came in second.

Even though Vanessa says not winning was disappointing, she realizes that doors have opened for her because of her involvement in cooking. Her prowess in the kitchen has taught her other things about herself too. "I may seem quiet. I might seem like the misfit," she says. "But I'm outgoing and very outspoken when it matters. Cooking has made me extraordinary."

Vanessa developed her **Spinach Smoothie** recipe as an homage to her newfound dedication to healthy eating. Spinach is iron-rich hero of the smoothie, but the combination of tart apples, kiwis, and lemon zest beautifully masks its woody flavor. The smoothie may be electric green, but the taste is all-natural sweetness and light.

(continued)

SPINACH SMOOTHIE

SERVES 4

½ cup water

2 cups lightly packed spinach

2 green apples, cored and chopped

2 kiwis, peeled and cubed

2 bananas

2 tablespoons grated lemon zest

½ cup cut-up honeydew melon

6 ounces low-fat vanilla yogurt

Combine all ingredients in a blender and process until smooth. Strain the smoothie through a fine-mesh sieve before serving. Serve cold.

Christopher Chernoff
Powell River, British Columbia, Canada

Bananas and soy or nut milk make 12-year-old vegan cook Christopher Chernoff's **Raspberry Smoothie** as creamy as the dairy version, while the dates offer depth of sweetness without refined sugar. He likes to have this smoothie when he's craving a sweet snack. For more about Christopher, see page 86.

RASPBERRY SMOOTHIE
SERVES 2 OR 3

1½ cups nondairy milk (soy, rice, almond, hemp, or coconut)

½ banana, frozen

½ cup vegan raspberry ice cream or raspberry sorbet

¼ teaspoon vanilla extract

½ cup orange juice

2 dates, pitted

1 cup fresh or frozen raspberries, plus a few extra for garnish

Combine all the ingredients in a blender and puree until smooth. Garnish with fresh or frozen raspberries.

Nondairy Milks

Milks made from almonds, rice, hemp, coconut, and soy are readily available in most mainstream grocery stores. For the most nutritional value, seek those that are fortified with the same complement of vitamins that cow's milk is—such as vitamin D. Those with gluten intolerances or allergies should read the labels on nondairy milks to ensure that no gluten-based thickening agent is used in the preparation.

Follow the FutureChefs

Catherine Amoriggi—*www.cookingwithcath.com*

Birke Baehr—*www.birkeonthefarm.com*

Deanna Baris—*www.dbandjelly.com*

Erica Barry—*www.cannella-vita.blogspot.com*

Logan Bello—*www.logansbites.com*

Nikita Bhuyan—*www.tastyhealthydishes.blogspot.com*

Alex and Sophia Biedny—*www.twokidscooking.com*

Kashia Cave—*www.mycitykitchen.com*

Allie Cerruti—*www.missjrchef.com*

Alessandra Ciuffo—*www.alessandraciuffo.com*

Madeline Dalton—*www.foodsforteensbyteens.blogspot.com*

Jess Dawson—*www.livininthekitchen.com*

Teddy Devico—*www.teenchefteddy.blogspot.com*

Abbie Emmons—*www.everythingneedssalt.com*

Drusilla Rose Falco—*www.teenagecakeland.wordpress.com*

Orren Fox—*www.happychickens.com*

Ben Gaiarin—*www.bengusto.com*

Logan Guleff—*www.orderupwithlogan.blogspot.com and www.barbequememphis.com*

Daniel Hamilton—*www.quiteabite.com*

Mazy Wirt Hanson—*www.mazysfoodadventures.blogspot.com*

Sunnie Heers—*www.moderngirlnutrition.com*

Sophia Hunt—*www.sophiasbaking.blogspot.com*

Mia Jessurun—*www.thelittlebluebicycle.blogspot.com.au*

Amber Kelley—*www.cookwithamber.com*

Amanda Koh Jia Yi—*www.crumbsandcookies.blogspot.sg*

Brooks Lange—*www.recipeboy.com*

Eliana de Las Casas—*www.kidchefeliana.com*

Sasha Meshcherekova—*www.teenchefinthekitchen.blogspot.ca*

Taylor Miller—*www.glutenaway.blogspot.com*

Katherine Murphy—*www.peanutbutterloving.blogspot.com*

Romilly Newman—*www.romillynewman.com*

Leah Newton—*www.onenerdbakery.blogspot.com*

Mason Partak—*www.masonpartak.com*

Alessandra Peters—*www.thefoodieteen.com*

Charles and Thomas Regnante—*www.2dudeswholovefood.blogspot.com*

Allison Schwartz—*www.bakingyear.com*

Remmi Anne Smith—*www.cooktimewithremmi.com*

Sophie Trachtenberg—*www.simplysophiebea.com*

Jack Witherspoon—*www.chefjackwitherspoon.com*

Index

Boldface page numbers indicate photographs. Underscored references indicate boxed text.